LINCOLN
Villages

Text by the Lincolnshire Federations of Women's Institutes
Photographs by Malcolm Sales

COUNTRYSIDE BOOKS
Newbury, Berkshire

First published 2002
© Photographs – Malcolm Sales 2002
© Text – Lincolnshire Federations of Women's Institutes 2002

COUNTRYSIDE BOOKS
3 Catherine Road
Newbury, Berkshire

To view our complete range of books,
please visit us at
www.countrysidebooks.co.uk

ISBN 1 85306 760 1

The front cover photograph shows Alford
the title page shows the dovecote at Belleau
and the back cover photograph shows Springthorpe

Designed by Graham Whiteman

Typeset by Techniset Typesetters, Newton-le-Willows
Produced through MRM Associates Ltd., Reading
Printed in Italy

FOREWORD

This all-colour book is a celebration of some of Lincolnshire's most photogenic villages. Along with superb pictures by landscape photographer Malcolm Sales, it brings together many of the accounts of village life contained in *The Lincolnshire Village Book*, first published in 1990.

Lincolnshire lies twixt the rolling wolds that border the Humber and the flat fens that surround the Wash. The focus is the city of Lincoln with its cathedral, university and castle. Rich Roman heritage is evident as illustrated by the recent significant artefacts unearthed in Ancaster (Roman name *Causenae*) and notably featured in the Channel 4 programme *Time Team*. In latter years the county became a home to the Royal Air Force, spawning many airfields, both permanent and wartime.

But the heart of Lincolnshire lies in its glorious villages. This book offers rural treasures in abundance and we heartily recommend it to you.

Anne Barns,
Chairman, Lincolnshire North Federation of Women's Institutes
Patricia Mundy,
Chairman, Lincolnshire South Federation of Women's Institutes
Autumn 2002

Winteringham

⌘ ABY

Aby bears the dual distinction of having the shortest place name in Lincolnshire and of occupying first place in any alphabetical listing for the county. The name of 'Aby' has its origins in the Old Norse word signifying water – 'Aby' is 'village by the water'. The water in question is that of the river Great Eau which flows through the village, providing the basis for a flourishing trout farm and the source of much good fishing. Footpaths following part of its course allow public enjoyment of this crystal clear water, its beauty enhanced by the presence of herons, geese, swans, a variety of ducks and the occasional kingfisher.

Aby (or Abi) was mentioned in the Domesday Book, its lands then being owned by Odo (Bishop of Bayeux and half brother of William the Conqueror) and Earl Hugh (Hugh the Wolf). At this time 27 acres of woodland were available for pannage (feeding swine) and it is interesting to note that at the edge of Aby there still exists 'Swinn Wood'.

Aby has an attractive location at the foot of the Lincolnshire Wolds and is formed almost in a square with a central playing field. Herbert Green in his *Village Life* descriptions written at the turn of the century called the area 'one of the prettiest parts of Lincolnshire' and made reference to the attractive gardens bordering the road through Aby. Aby is fortunate also to possess several stretches of ancient hedgerow supporting a rich variety of flora and fauna.

The northern entry into Aby is marked by an old girder bridge, part of the East Lincolnshire branch of the London and North Eastern Railway. The line was completed in 1848 and since its closure in 1970 has become something of a private nature reserve.

⌘ ALFORD

There was a settlement here at Alford in pre-Norman times but the importance of the village's situation was recognised when William of Well became lord of the manor. Alford church was built in the 1350s on the site of an earlier building. There is a very fine 14th century wooden screen and a richly carved dark oak Jacobean pulpit. Alford still has a beautiful fully operational five-sailed windmill built in 1813 of brick, tarred over to ensure that it was waterproof. It is painted white and is visible for many miles. Around Alford are many small villages and hamlets with interesting buildings.

At Haugh a line of very ancient yew trees leads to a farmhouse built on the site of an old mansion. Close by is a tiny ancient stone church with a Norman doorway. Well village overlooks a lake and a park which leads to a small church built in 1733 to resemble a Grecian temple.

Ulceby is a small village on the banks of a stream. A red brick church with a bellcote also serves the hamlet of Fordington where the humps of a 'lost village'

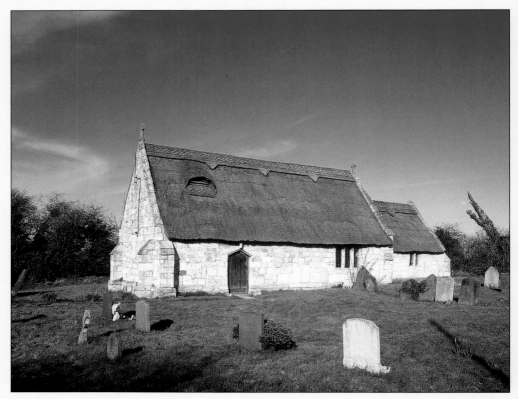

Markby's little thatched church of St Peter

can be seen. At Claxby two long barrows are clearly visible. One has been much damaged by a chalk pit, now owned by the Lincolnshire Wildlife Trust, as is the nearby Hoplands Wood.

Willoughby lies on the edge of the marsh. There are interesting modern windows in the ancient church depicting the life of Captain John Smith, who was born in the village in 1579. He emigrated to America, where his life was saved by Pocahontas.

Bilsby is a fast growing village with a much restored church. The tower has old brick battlements. Markby is the site of an old Augustinian (Black Friars) priory. The little thatched church has box pews and fragments of early stonework. At Hagnaby there was once a Premonstratensian (White Friars) priory, fragments of which remain at the nearby farm.

A tiny greenstone Georgian church can be found at Hannah, on the last piece of rising ground before the coast. Belleau also has a greenstone church, greatly rebuilt in the 19th century but containing the remains of a much older building and an effigy of a crosslegged knight.

⌘ ALLINGTON

In old documents the name of the village is spelled Adelington or Athelyngton, indicating that it was a Saxon settlement. Its name means the home of the family of Athel, a Northumbrian prince.

From Domesday until recent times it was a combination of two parishes, East and West Allington, supporting two Anglican churches and a Methodist chapel.

St James's church, which was always connected with the neighbouring village of Sedgebrook, was demolished in 1947. All that now remains is the graveyard and a stone cross erroneously marked 'St Andrew's'. The Methodist chapel was demolished in 1938. The present parish church of Holy Trinity, originally of West Allington, displays a variety of architectural styles demonstrating repairs and extensions over the centuries. The poet, George Crabbe, was rector here from 1790 to 1814.

The village was owned by the Welby family for nearly 200 years, hence the name of the public house, and changed very little until the estate was sold after the Second World War.

The Green at Sedgebrook

The cross on the village green is a market cross, Allington at one time having been second only in importance to Grantham as a market.

On the Sedgebrook road is a stone-capped chalybeate spring known as the Salt Well. Before the mains water supply was connected this was an important source of water for farm stock.

Today the population of over 500 is served by a church, a school, a general store-cum-post office, a public house and a village hall, and, situated between the A1 and A52, the village gives easy access to many large cities.

⌘ ANTON'S GOWT

Slightly to the north-west of Boston lies the village of Anton's Gowt, reached via the B1184. The word 'gowt' means sluice, but the more common name locally is Anton's Gowt Lock. This is a haunt for both anglers and boating enthusiasts, many of whom frequent the river Witham and the Oak Tree public house.

There have always been many different forms of business in the community. In the past there was the Malcolm Arms (now the Oak Tree), the railway, village shop, petrol pump, milk and paper rounds. Now there are kennels, a dog and cat cemetery, potteries and a game farm, plus many other businesses.

Anton's Gowt, looking north along the river Witham

The almshouses and memorial to the 9th Squadron RAF, Bardney

The Lincoln to Boston boat race, held annually, attracts local and far off visitors, many coming to support a particular crew. Ideally, summer is the best time in the village, as most people are very keen gardeners, and the flowers are a sheer delight.

⌘ BARDNEY

The question 'Do you come from Bardney?' means not 'Are you a Bardneyite?' but is a way of saying 'You've left the door open', referring to a legend from Bardney's 7th century abbey, the resting place of King Ethelred of Mercia. After the monks of Bardney Abbey had closed their door to the bones of the saint and martyr Oswald, they received a wrathful divine message by a pillar of light and they vowed never to close the door again! This abbey was restored by Gilbert of Ghent in 1087 and devastated by Henry VIII in 1538.

The village stands at a crossroads looking westwards over the fens to Lincoln Cathedral and eastwards to the Wolds and coast, surrounded by rich agricultural land.

Bardney and its hamlet Southrey are now home to some 2,000 people and was once dominated by the British Sugar factory, which processed half a million tonnes of sugar beet during the season.

The 15th century church of St Laurence, the early 18th century Handcock's Almshouse and Kitching's Charity School and school house are at the centre of the village around the green, with the addition of an appropriate memorial to the 9th Squadron of the Royal Air Force who were stationed here during the Second World War.

⌘ BARKSTON LE WILLOWS

Barkston le Willows is an attractive village lying on the river Witham four miles north-east of Grantham. Mentioned in the Domesday Book in 1086, the village at that time was called Barchester. The survey listed a Roman camp and four mills in the area.

The church of St Nicholas is on the site of previous churches, dating back 700 years. In 1837 a free school was opened in the village, although there already existed a small school, the gift of the Newton family, for six poor children, dating from the 17th century.

The church of St Nicholas, Barkston le Willows

In recent years there have been a number of new houses built but the old village still stays the same with a thriving village hall.

In November a Craft Fair is held in the village hall which attracts a great number of local people.

⌘ BELTON

Belton is a picturesque village, three and a half miles from Grantham, boasting Tudor bedehouses.

Belton House was designed by Sir Christopher Wren and completed by James Wyatt in 1685 and was the home of the Brownlow family for almost 300 years. Lord Brownlow was Lord in Waiting to Edward VIII and some of the souvenirs on display in the house relate to the abdication in 1936. The house, which is surrounded by beautiful parkland, is now owned by the National Trust and is open from Easter to October each year. For the visitor there are nature trails and an adventure playground for the children amongst the delights to enjoy.

Belton's picturesque village street

Many memorials of the Brownlow family can be found in the church of St Peter and St Paul, the tower of which dates from about 1200.

On the outskirts of the village is Bridgewater House, which was at one time the home of the Fitzherbert Wrights, grandparents to Sarah, the Duchess of York.

A most delightful garden centre is situated in Belton which attracts many visitors from miles around.

⌘ BINBROOK

Binbrook is in an idyllic setting in the North Lincolnshire Wolds, mentioned in the

The village waterpump, Binbrook

Domesday Book as Binnibroc. The population peaked in 1861 at 1,334 and has continually declined since. The village once had a weekly market but records refer to this being sold to Caistor many years ago.

The village was noted for the purity of its water in the 19th century and for being built on a brook abounding with trout. The brook, which flowed through pasture between the manor and the church, was piped in in 1989 to allow for building development.

The parish church of St Mary and St Gabriel was consecrated in 1869 and united the two former parishes. St Gabriel's, its churchyard now grassed over, makes a pleasant quiet corner in which to sit. St Mary's, a small plain structure, was pulled down in 1867. The present church is often referred to as the 'cathedral on the Wolds'.

Methodist gatherings began with open air meetings and in private buildings. The quaint Ranters chapel still stands, since used as a garage and workshop. The Wesleyan, Primitive and the Free Methodist chapels also have other uses. The present Wesleyan chapel was built in 1877.

The hill farmers depended on the village for drinking water and Cornelius Stovin in his *Journals of a Methodist Farmer 1871 – 1875* noted that his men went down to the village for water. The pump on the Grimsby Road was built on a ramp to enable water carts to fill up.

Life in earlier times was centred round the Market Place, High Street and Back Lane with their blacksmiths, beerhouses, builders, bakers and millers, carpenters, carriers, ropery, reading room, shops, shoemakers, tailors and wheelwrights. The white cottage in the Market Place with a cartwheel outside denotes the premises of Mr Walt Appleton – wheelwright, carpenter and undertaker. A market trap built in 1899, owned and used by Mr Robert Stark, carrier, was restored by students from the Lincolnshire College of Art conservation course and is now displayed in the transport gallery of the Museum of Lincolnshire Life.

⌘ BLYTON

Blyton is a long narrow village occupying more than a mile of the busy A159 Gainsborough-Scunthorpe road.

Parts of the church, dedicated to St Martin, date from Norman times, though its most unusual feature is the collection of the flags of the Allies in the First World War. At the end of the war in 1918 the vicar wrote to each nation requesting its flag; the letters received in reply have been retained, including the one from Buckingham Palace explaining that the Royal Standard could only be displayed when the King was present so his request must be refused!

The popular children's authoress, Enid Blyton, was descended from the local de Bilton family, who were wealthy wool merchants.

Blyton

⌘ BRACEBOROUGH

Braceborough in rural Lincolnshire is reached only by narrow lanes. It boasts its own spa, where once Spa House had its spa room for taking the water. At one time the water was bottled and sold.

King George III is rumoured to have taken the water and to have been treated by Francis Willis MD who resided at Braceborough Hall. Dr Willis ran a private asylum for mentally ill people at Shillingthorpe, an ancient and remote hamlet of Braceborough.

It is believed Dr Willis kept his trap in the stone trap hovel at the entrance to Manor Farm. A trap hovel is so called because it has doors either end. One drove into the trap hovel with both doors open and led the pony out at the front leaving the trap inside the building.

The friendly village community is served by St Margaret's church. The village hall was once the school and was built by the Willis family in 1870 and left in trust, 'to be used for the education of adults and children of the labouring, manufacturing and other poorer classes in the parish of Braceborough'.

⌘ BRANSTON

Branston, which dates from Saxon times, is situated in open countryside four miles from Lincoln on the B1188 to Sleaford and its centre is the old village with winding lanes and stone-built cottages. There are many well-walked country footpaths with views of the Wolds and the cathedral, and a guide to these can be bought from the local library.

The village is well catered for in terms of schools, playgroups, evening classes and recreational activities. The new village hall was opened in 1981 and is situated in the extensive recreation field which includes tennis courts, football and cricket pitches, a bowling green and a children's play area.

The tower of All Saints' church was built by the Saxons and there are some interesting pew ends, one of which has a carving of a pig playing the famous Lincolnshire bagpipes. For 211 continuous years a member of the Curtois family was the incumbent and there are three former rectories, one of which has a cock-fighting pit in its garden.

There are two Halls: the first, which was built in 1735, burned down in 1903 whilst the annual Goose Supper was being enjoyed at the second, new Hall.

The village pub in Branston with All Saint's church beyond

The picturesque stream which flows through the village is home to many ducks and the occasional trout. This stream provided the power for the former waterworks with a huge waterwheel which pumped the water to the large houses. The wheel is still in existence.

⌘ BRANT BROUGHTON

Brant Broughton lies near the foot of the Lincoln Cliff, and its church spire, one of the most elegant in the county, draws visitors like a magnet. Along the High Street and scattered down the lanes where wide verges once provided grazing, are some fine brick and stone houses. They date mainly from the 18th century, and several incorporated much earlier and humbler dwellings, which then became the kitchen quarters as their owners moved up the social scale.

St Helen's church is described by Henry Thorold in *Lincolnshire Churches* as 'without doubt one of the most glorious of all Lincolnshire churches . . . like a medieval dream.' It has a number of carvings, some of which were regarded by a contributor to the *Gentleman's Magazine* in February 1809 as 'too indelicate to be permitted to occupy one of your plates'.

The Quaker meeting house was originally a thatched barn belonging to Thomas Robinson. He and his family fled here from London in 1665 to escape the plague. Meetings of Quakers were held illegally and Robinson had some of his property seized as a punishment for attending them. By 1701 the laws against Dissenters had been suspended for some years, and Robinson and his wife Sarah gave their barn for use as a meeting house. Their initials may still be seen above the door.

Education was first provided for poor children in the village in 1731. In 1852 and 1871, the Methodists and the Church of England respectively established their own all-age mixed schools, and there was considerable rivalry between them. The log books of both schools tell of the problem of poor attendance. The rector at the Church school attempted to improve the situation. On Friday afternoons he gave a metal token to every child with a full week's attendance. At the end of the year the tokens were each redeemed for one old penny. In 1898 this cost him over £8 and another year over £10.

⌘ BURGH LE MARSH

Burgh le Marsh is a thriving community, constantly expanding with new developments, situated a few miles west of Skegness on the A158.

Outdoor activities consist of football, cricket, bowls, fishing and a Rifle and Pistol Club. For those who enjoy walking there are many pleasant walks along country roads and field paths. Recently a picnic area has been provided at the Grand Pits. At the village hall there is something going on nearly every evening, and the venue has proved so popular that the old schoolhouse was bought as an

Burgh

annexe. This includes a new library. There is also a windmill which is operated in the summer with voluntary help.

Amenities include a school, post office, garages, a dairy, a doctor's surgery, a library, a coal merchant's, several public houses and various shops. There is a library service for the housebound and meals on wheels. There are two rest homes for the elderly, Burgh Hall and St Paul's. More dwelling houses are being put up as the population increases and a new school has been built for the same reason. Flats now stand where once the old cattle market used to be.

There are three places of worship in Burgh. The parish church, dedicated to St Peter & St Paul, is an impressive building of Portland stone, with a fine tower.

⌘ CAISTOR

Caistor is situated high on a western spur of the Wolds, off the A46 between Great Grimsby and Market Rasen. It is a place of steep, narrow, winding lanes, of flights of steps and little passageways and of magnificent views, including that of Lincoln Cathedral in the far distance.

The Victorian village pump with its coat of arms, Caistor

Caistor was a Roman camp and many vestiges of the Roman occupation have been found. Parts of the wall which surrounded the camp are still in existence and Ermine Street passes nearby. Another important road is the ancient High Street which runs from Caistor to Horncastle.

Caistor men were involved in the Lincolnshire Rising of 1536, which was a reaction against Henry VIII's attacks on the Church, and there is an effigy of Sir Edward Maddison, who played a prominent part in the rising, in the church of St Peter and St Paul. This beautiful church is of the Norman and Early English periods. The glass and nearly all of the church plate is modern and the church houses a Gad Whip. The whip is connected with a custom that took place on Palm Sundays in the past whereby a whip, a purse containing silver and some pieces of wych elm had to be presented at Matins.

The Market Place is most interesting, having several late 17th and 18th century buildings. There are no earlier buildings due to the 'great fire' in 1681. The many different roof levels add charm and character as does the Victorian pump with its coat of arms. The gems of Caistor are its fresh water springs, Syfer Spring in Fountain Street perhaps being the best.

⌘ CAYTHORPE WITH FRIESTON

Caythorpe with Frieston is a very friendly village on the A607 within easy reach of Lincoln, Grantham, Sleaford and Newark. The surrounding countryside is pleasant and varied and there are many picturesque houses with colourful attractive gardens.

The village is fortunate to have an abundance of amenities. There are two mini-supermarkets, a butcher's shop, a fish and chip shop which also delivers fresh fish, a post office, a school, a church, public houses which also serve food, a surgery and three resident doctors, a garage, a hairdresser, a dressmaker and Margaret's Studio featuring hand-painted china. Residing in the village are plumbers and decorators, builders and electricians – to name but a few.

At one end of the village is a complex of warden-controlled bungalows with an adjacent community centre. Near to the church is a residential home for the elderly. The village hall is used to capacity for various social events and there is a spacious playing field with a large pavilion for the cricket and football clubs – a children's play area is also incorporated.

Near to the village is Caythorpe Agricultural College which provides various courses throughout the year. Plants, pot plants, cut flowers and farm produce are available for sale to the public.

⌘ CHAPEL-ST-LEONARDS

Chapel-St-Leonards is a popular holiday spot

Chapel-St-Leonards is a 'village-by-the-sea' with an extensive sandy beach and a real village green. It is a few miles north of Skegness, off the A520.

It has a Women's Institute, a branch of the Royal British Legion and several other recreational organisations.

The Methodist chapel and St Leonard's parish church – which is thought to have the only red-towered spire in the country – provide for the religious needs of a population of around 2,700.

Several pubs, two hotels a good variety of shops and an octagonal village hall complete the picture. The village hall was provided by public subscription and is 'managed' by a committee elected annually.

Upwards of 50,000 visitors come to Chapel-St-Leonards each year, proving its popularity as a holiday village, particularly for families with children.

⌘ CHERRY WILLINGHAM

Cherry Willingham lies three miles east of Lincoln on the south-facing slope above the wide valley of the river Witham. Lincolnshire has several Willinghams so our village has Cherry as the first part of its name, probably because there was once an orchard called Cherry Holt just below the church.

The village has spread outwards from the original settlement behind the church, where Iron Age remains have been found. A series of long narrow medieval fishponds is still in existence. A Roman villa was discovered just above the flood plain of the Witham, which was not embanked until late Victorian times.

The fen is the source of bog oak, large trees dragged out of their graves in the peat and hauled away to the clay soil for safe burning. If the fen peat is set alight it can smoulder for weeks.

At the time of the Domesday survey there was a church and a priest and two fisheries worth 32 pence yearly. After the Conquest the manor was owned by the Marmion family until the early 18th century when it passed into the ownership of Thomas Becket, whose memorial is in the church. The church of St Peter and St Paul, an excellent example of Georgian architecture was consecrated in 1753. It is built of high quality Ancaster limestone and stands on a commanding mound.

Cherry Willingham is twinned with Le Grand Luce, a small town near Le Mans. Coach parties of French or English make the 350 mile journey to stay with their host families and enjoy a contrasting style of life. Lasting friendships have been formed and as a result we have come to know each other better.

⌘ COLSTERWORTH WITH WOOLSTHORPE

The villages of Colsterworth and Woolsthorpe lie half a mile to the west of the A1, seven miles south of Grantham and 13 miles north of Stamford. Colsterworth is raised upon a slight limestone ridge with the river Witham running below on the western side and bisecting the two villages. The ancient village of Twyford has been engulfed by the expansion of Colsterworth to the south but the name is preserved in the names of certain houses. At one time before the bypass was built, Colsterworth lay astride the Great North Road.

The nucleus of the village lies along the High Street where, in the hey-day of the coaching trade, there were numerous inns, ten at one time. The White Lion alone now serves the population, standing opposite the parish church of St John the Baptist, the origins of which go back to Saxon times, as indicated by the herring-bone stonework in the chancel. The fine Norman arches were preserved during the Victorian period of renovation, of which this church is an outstanding example.

Although the oldest dwellings are of limestone, brick homes of the 1920s and 1930s are interposed amongst them, giving the village a rather patchy appearance.

Woolsthorpe, although attached to Colsterworth by administration, has a character all its own, being smaller and quieter. It is famous as the birthplace of Sir Isaac Newton in 1642. His home, Woolsthorpe Manor, attracts visitors from all over the world. The village hall was built as a result of an appeal in his memory and is named after him. He was christened in the church of St John the Baptist, where a copy of the entry in the register is to be seen.

⌘ CONINGSBY

Coningsby is a large, thriving village on the A153 Midlands to East Coast road. It is within easy reach of Horncastle, Boston, Sleaford and Lincoln. The river Bain flows alongside the village, which is on the edge of the Lincolnshire Fens. In the Domesday survey, Coningsby was a prosperous place with ten fisheries.

St Michael's church is famous for its one-handed clock, fascinating to horologists, as the $16\frac{1}{2}$ ft painted dial, pre-mid 17th century, is reputed to be the largest of its kind in the world. The unusual mechanism consists of hand-crafted iron wheels, stone weights and steel ropes.

Although a church probably existed here pre-Conquest, the tower on which the clock is painted is 15th century. This tower is unusual in that it stands outside of the church, with a beautifully arched carriageway underneath and an unglazed rose window to the west.

The Royal Air Force station, Coningsby, is the base of Tornado aeroplanes of Strike Command, the first line of defence. Plane spotters converge around the perimeter of the Royal Air Force station at Coningsby to pursue their hobby, as aircraft of many kinds and countries come and go.

The Battle of Britain Memorial Flight is housed on the airfield, manned by volunteer former fliers, and is open Mondays to Fridays to the public. Thousands of people flock to the RAF Open Day each year, in June. Proceeds are shared among various local charities.

Many leisure activities are catered for by various groups. Cruises to Boston or Lincoln may be taken from Belle Isle on the river Witham. There are quiet roads for horse riders and walks of various distances along river banks or by fields.

⌘ CORBY GLEN

Corby Glen – the name formally adopted in 1955 to avoid confusion with the town of Corby, Northants – is a village of approximately 450 inhabitants, situated on the Bourne-Colsterworth road. The village and surrounding parish of 2,799 acres are situated in wooded hilly countryside in a largely farming area.

During the redecoration of St John's church in 1939 discovery was made of a remarkable series of wall paintings, said to be the finest in Lincolnshire. In medieval times few men could read or write and it was common practice to illustrate stories from the bible by paintings on the church walls. As progress was made from one story to the next the paintings would be covered with whitewash and further pictures painted on top.

The Willoughby Memorial Gallery and Museum is housed in what was formerly a free grammar school. A trust was founded in 1965 by the Earl of

The market square at Corby Glen

The three-arch bridge at Deeping St James

Ancaster in memory of his son who was drowned in the Mediterranean. There is a well stocked library and reading room and several times a year exhibitions of art and related subjects are staged for the public.

Perhaps Corby Glen is best known for its annual sheep fair, which owes its origin to a Royal Charter of 1238. At one time sheep were brought in by rail and on foot from as far away as Suffolk, Oxfordshire and the Scottish border. The fair was a notable event in the calendar, being at the end of the farming financial year (tenant farmers in hard times would be forced to sell their sheep in order to settle rent arrears). Over the years there has been a decline in the number of sheep brought to auction at the October Fair, but it is still an occasion when reunions of families and friends take place. October 1988 saw the 750th anniversary of this event and a week of displays and celebrations took place.

⌘ DEEPING ST JAMES

In 1220 Est Depinge was granted a charter for a market to be held on the high ground on the western side, where now the modern roads A15 and A16 meet; so the two villages of Market Deeping and Deeping St James were formed.

Deeping St James took its name from the priory church of St James and St Benedict, which was founded in 1139 by Baldwin FitzGilbert, Norman lord of the manor. The village green and lock-up must be two of the smallest in the county. The lock-up, now known as the Cross, is a small square building, once used as a meeting room and later on to house village drunks.

The river Welland was used as a highway for trade when barges went their way to Stamford and Market Deeping. Along Bridge Street, just before the locks, there is an old house with a canal window on its first storey, used to sight the traffic on the river. The river has always played a part in the social life of the village – in the 1930s the Bathing Belles, led by District Nurse Lanham, believed in a daily dip for health; today there are canoe races, duck (plastic) races for charity and tug-of-war contests across it.

In the Linch Field along the Spalding road a Bronze Age cinerary urn was found, which is now in the British Museum. There are many links with Roman times, including the Car Dyke crossing with the river Welland.

The road to Peterborough and the south goes over the river by the old three-arch bridge, which is very narrow and has small niches each side for pedestrians to step into to avoid the traffic. Along Bridge Street, by the bridge, is the Cave Abdullam Baptist church, founded by Reverend F. Tyron, a former vicar at the church, who disagreed with Church doctrines and built and endowed his own place of worship.

⌘ DEEPING ST NICHOLAS

The village of Deeping St Nicholas in south Lincolnshire is one of the longest villages in the country, extending some five miles along the busy A16 south of Spalding.

The name Deeping means 'a place in the deep meadows, subject to flooding' and the parish of St Nicholas in Deeping Fen lies so low that it would not exist without a careful system of drainage. Efforts to keep the water away extend from the reign of Queen Elizabeth I when a petition was presented to drain the fens. During the 1630s the Earl of Bedford and Sir Philibert Vernatti carried out much effective work in draining the area with the cutting of Vernatts Drain and Counter Drain, and the improvement of North and South Drove Drains. Windmill pumps met with only partial success and it was not until the establishment of steam pumps in the mid 1800s that an efficient drainage system was obtained. This work is continued today by an electric pumping station at Pode Hole.

With the proper drainage of the fens in 1845 a church was built and dedicated to St Nicholas and this gave its name to the village. The parish church was designed by the Sleaford architect, Charles Kirk, in the style of the mid 14th century with a dramatic spire, and built of Ancaster stone. It has a peal of six bells. There is also a thriving Methodist church, built in 1867.

The parish of Deeping St Nicholas includes the small village of Tongue End which is some seven miles away by road. Here, during prolonged periods of hard frost, land adjacent to the river Glen is flooded and ice skating championships held.

⌘ DENTON

Denton was part of the land granted by William the Conqueror to his Standard Bearer, Robert de Todenni – hence the name Denton. The original village was built around the church and village green (now the garden of Denton House). Park Lane is said to have been the first village street, and its continuation can still be traced through the park.

Lincolnshire is usually associated with flat country, but Denton, which is a delightful cluster of buildings, is in a sheltered vale and cosily situated in a corner of South Lincolnshire. The Main Street calls for the engagement of a low gear and Church Street too rises gently, with St Andrew's church crowning its highest point.

The Norman church is built of the local 'yellow' stone, and when floodlit by the sun St Andrew's is a magnificent golden building. On entering the church, the many stained glass windows throw warm welcoming shadows across the aisles, and the soft furnishings (a serene blue in colour) are very pleasing to the eye. The registers date from 1558, and nowadays the rector is shared with three other parishes.

The nearest market town is Grantham to the east, with Melton Mowbray to the west. Re-entering Denton from Grantham, the first view is of the ornate gatehouses standing guard over Denton Manor House drive; these were built in 1898.

This ornate gatehouse stands guard over Denton Manor House

The village was once part of the Forest of Kesteven, and trees are still a feature of Denton, many of which grow to a great height. Many new trees have been planted and these too are showing remarkable growth. The horse chestnuts are particularly beautiful in Denton and visitors come to enjoy their glorious blossoms each June.

⌘ DONINGTON

Donington, once a small but thriving market town in the Lincolnshire Fens, lies almost equidistant from Spalding and Boston and is inhabited by around 2,500 people. Now designated a major village, it was referred to as Donnictune in the Domesday Book. Then a hamlet, its salt works were worth £1 per year and land was valued at 60 shillings. Its prosperity in the Middle Ages is evident from the size and grandeur of the church.

Australians visit St Mary and the Holy Rood throughout the year to pay homage to their hero, Captain Matthew Flinders RN. His memorial is in the church and, since 1980, thanks largely to the generosity of the Australian Governors, a stained glass window commemorates his exploits. Matthew, son of the local doctor, is said to have been fired with a desire to go to sea after reading *Robinson Crusoe*. Fearful of voicing this ambition to a disapproving father, he printed his request on to the surgery slate! He was the first person to circumnavigate Australia and bestowed many Lincolnshire place names on that land. During his 40 year life span he achieved a great deal and endured much hardship including over six years captivity on Mauritius during the course of his explorations.

In commemoration of Captain Flinders, the heads of all the Australian States make an annual pilgrimage to Lincolnshire in early March.

The Market Place is surrounded by shops supplying every commodity to a growing community. At the end of the High Street stands Cowley's School, established in 1719 by Thomas Cowley, the village's greatest benefactor.

Situated in the heart of Tulipland, Donington holds an annual Flower Festival timed to coincide with Spalding's Flower Parade. The church is decorated and hundreds of meals are served to the travel-weary by volunteers.

⌘ EAST KEAL

East Keal is about two miles south of Spilsby along the A16, on the edge of the Lincolnshire Wolds and fens. The village dates back to Saxon times, and the site to the Stone Age. It is still a farming village with sheep in the Wolds fields and crops on the fens, very much as it has always been. It is only the views that have changed. The wild marsh and meers of the fens are now a flat patchwork of fields and the odd line of trees for a windbreak, with buildings scattered here and there.

Mavis Enderby is just a pleasant stroll away from East Keal

On the edge of the village to the east there is an ancient well, on the border with Hundleby. It is called the Virgin's Well and has never been known to dry up, very important in earlier times. It is much covered over now and hidden in the Twentylands Plantation. It is a pleasant place to go for a walk, one of a number around the village, taking in the fields and hedgerows of the Wolds and the ditches and dykes of the fens, all rich in wildlife.

If one decides to take a walk up the hill towards Old Bolingbroke and Mavis Enderby and then looks back, the view is really quite breathtaking. On a clear day one can see as far as the coast, and you can also see the churches of eight parishes from this spot. Just by the lane end there is a road sign that used to say 'To Old Bolingbroke and Mavis Enderby', to which a wit with a spray can had added 'a Son'. It has gone now.

⌘ FISHTOFT

A rapidly expanding village lying two miles east-south-east of Boston. The name of this parish is written in the Domesday Book as Toft. 'Toft' is generally understood

The memorial to the Pilgrim Fathers at Fishtoft

to imply a hill or higher ground, which correctly applies to this parish when compared with the surrounding countryside.

The 19th century local historian Pishey Thompson states in his account of Fishtoft that a creek of considerable magnitude once flowed from near the church to the neighbourhood of the present Hob Hole Pumping Station, and clear traces of this creek can still be seen to the east of the Cut End Road.

Apart from its beautiful church dedicated to St Guthlac, Fishtoft has only one historic building still standing, Rochford Tower. This fortified manor house was built in the early 16th century. Sometimes known as Kyme Tower (members of the Kyme family are buried in Fishtoft church) it is an impressive red brick tower with corner turrets and embattled parapet. It is supposed that the present tower stands on or near the site of the ancient Richmond Tower of Fenne.

The Rochford family can be traced back to the Norman Conquest. Alan Rufus, Earl of Brittany and Richmond, a nephew of William the Conqueror, was the first subject in the Kingdom of England and next in rank to the Royal Family.

Towards the southern end of the village is the site of a monument to the memory of the Pilgrim Fathers who attempted to sail from Boston to Holland in order to find more favourable scope for their particular religious views. In 1620 came the historic journey of the Pilgrim Fathers to America – vanguard of a great tide of migration in which the town of Boston was to be closely involved.

⌘ FISKERTON

Fiskerton borders the northern bank of the river Witham five miles east of Lincoln. The Domesday Book mentions three fisheries at Fiskerton, an indication that the village received its name as 'home of the fishermen' in ancient times. Recent excavations by archaeologists unearthed substantial remains of a wooden pier and several bone needles undoubtedly used in repairing nets, which have been dated back to the Stone Age. A wooden canoe, a large cache of axe heads and medieval jewellery have also been discovered, proving thousands of years of continuing habitation.

In this county of memorable old churches, Fiskerton boasts a splendid example dedicated to St Clement where Christians have worshipped for a thousand years.

Particularly attractive in the summer time when yellow water lilies abound along the village stretch, the river, running alongside the entire length of the

The iron pedestrian bridge over the Witham river, Fiskerton

parish, is a popular spot for anglers, walkers and nature lovers. Here too an iron pedestrian bridge provides the only crossing of the river between Lincoln and Bardney. Fiskerton is noted as having one of the few known ponds in Great Britain where the Great Crested Newt breeds.

RAF Fiskerton opened in 1943 and was home to 49 Squadron RAF. The station closed in 1945 and then became the Lincolnshire headquarters of the Royal Observer Corps. Little remains of the wartime airfield now, apart from short lengths of runway.

It is believed that the saying 'Getting the wrong end of the stick' originated in Fiskerton centuries ago when it was the custom for land to be conveyed between the steward and tenant at the manor court by each grasping one end of a 6 ft long pole.

⌘ FOTHERBY

Fotherby lies off the A16 road between Grimsby and Louth at the foot of the Lincolnshire Wolds. Approaching the village from either the north or south one's first view is of the broach spire of St Mary's church, which dominates the

These six almshouses at Fotherby were built by Everitt Allenby in 1867

village. The church was built in 1863 on the site of an earlier church, the walls are of chalk and sandstone lined inside with red bricks and sandstone bands. There is a 15th century font, a medieval piscina and three 17th century bells.

The six almshouses have long been a feature of the village. Built on the site of an old vicarage in 1867 by the generosity of Everitt Allenby, they have provided sheltered housing for over 120 years. The exterior of the almshouses has not been altered, though the interiors are now modernised.

Everitt Allenby was born at Manor Farm in 1794. He later left the village for London where he became a successful businessman. He died in 1868. He provided money for the chancel of St Mary's church when it was built in 1863.

Fotherby is a village most people glide past on the recently opened by-pass. If the traveller leaves the main road and takes the country lane to Fotherby Top, 350 ft high, on a clear day his journey will be rewarded by the most wonderful views of the long stretch of marshland and of the sea as far as the Humber and Spurn Head.

Linger a while by the common, a peaceful spot to enjoy the sights and sounds of nature in the countryside on a summer day.

⌘ FRAMPTON

Frampton is four miles south of Boston. A noticeable feature of this fen village is its trees. No other village around the Wash can boast so many.

At Mill Hill crossroads the copse is a colourful sight in springtime with snowdrops and daffodils. To the west, behind a brick wall, is Frampton House, built in 1792 by the Tunnard family. The poor road conditions from here to the parish church, and the distance involved, resulted in the Tunnards building St Michael's church in 1863.

On Ralphs Lane a commemorative plate marks the site of the gibbet where in 1792 Ralph Smith was the last person to be hung in chains in the Boston area. He had murdered Gentle Sutton.

Frampton Hall, standing in its own park, was built in 1725 by Coney Tunnard. Rabbits appear on many parts of the buildings and railings as a pun on his name. (See the rabbit on the chandelier he gave to the church.) The house was built with three storeys, uncommon at that time. The later east wing has the arms of the Moore family who married into the Tunnard family.

St Mary's church is mentioned in the Domesday survey. The earliest parts are the tower and broach spire which are late 12th century. The earliest gravestone dates from 1693 and is near the east window.

The Greenwich Meridian is crossed on the way to the sea banks and salt marshes. Frampton Marsh is a bird sanctuary. A local delicacy growing here is samphire. Boiled and pickled in vinegar it is eaten with cold ham.

St Mary's church, Frampton, with its broach spire

⌘ FRISKNEY

Friskney is a large and widely scattered coastal parish some 13 miles north of Boston and eight miles south of Skegness. It borders upon the Wash and is situated between the marsh and the fens. It has not always been by the sea, and at low tide the remains of a prehistoric forest can be seen. The remains of a Stone Age camp have also been found. Behind the sea bank, known as the Roman Bank, traces of the Roman salt pans can still be seen.

At some time following the Roman withdrawal the first church, dedicated to St Katherine of Alexandria, was built at Abbey Hills. It lasted through the Danish occupation, when Friskney was a southernmost part of the Danelaw. Then came the Normans and Friskney passed to the de Kyme family. To them we probably owe the first church of All Saints which was begun in 1135. The lower part of the tower is all that is left of the original building, then it passes through Early English and Perpendicular stages. It houses six bells and a clock and is entered by a magnificent arch.

Friskney's lot during the Civil War was not an enviable one – Cromwell's forces held Boston while Wainfleet was for the King, and Friskney had to help both sides in money and kind as well as sending men to fight and guard Wainfleet's 'Salem Bridge'.

Since the 14th century efforts had been made to drain the land, for much of the parish was under water for six months of the year. This was bitterly opposed by the inhabitants but in 1809, by a special Act of Parliament, drainage at last began and Friskney quickly changed. As the land reclamation went on, potatoes were the main crop. These were sent by rail to the London and Yorkshire markets. During the latter part of last century market gardening came into its own and large lorries, some of which go as far afield as Europe, transport fresh vegetables.

⌘ FRITHVILLE

Two hundred and fifty years ago the parish of Frithville was unenclosed marshland on the edge of the West Fen. In the 13th century monks from Kirkstead Abbey grazed their immense flocks of sheep on 500 acres of the Frith. In the summer the Frith would be white with the number of sheep; in the winter, when the marsh became swamp, the inhabitants made their living by fishing and wildfowling.

Several attempts had been made to drain the marsh and nearby fenlands, but were unsuccessful until the 19th century, when corn was needed to feed the army horses in the Napoleonic Wars. Sir Joseph Banks was an important promoter of the project. Parliament passed the necessary Acts and, in spite of the local people's objections, the work went ahead and Frith became intersected by man-made drains. One cuts the village into two parts, and is now lined by trees planted to mark the Silver Jubilee of George V and the Coronation of George VI.

Roads were built on the banks of the waterways. Beautiful brick bridges were constructed, high enough for the packet boats to pass underneath on their way to Boston market. The men who had been fen slodgers became agricultural labourers working for yeoman farmers who owned their small farms.

Frith became Frithville, a village with a windmill to grind corn for making bread and animal foodstuffs which were delivered locally by horse and cart.

Under the Enclosure Act a fund was created for the building and maintenance of fen chapels – Frithville's was built in 1821 and dedicated to St Peter. Then, in 1899, a Methodist chapel was built. The congregations of St Peter's and the chapel have now joined an ecumenical partnership.

Although Frithville is not a picturesque village attracting tourists its people do enjoy magnificent cloudscapes, beautiful sunsets and clear starlit nights. In summer it is a land of plenty: in winter, when the flat fields stretch under an overcast sky to the horizon, and the lonely cry of the peewit is heard at dusk, you may well have the feeling that the days when all was marsh are not so very far away.

⌘ FULSTOW

Fulstow – 'Fugelstow' – is mentioned in the Domesday Book and is said to mean the home of a hermit. The village is eight miles north of Louth and is a pleasant place of approximately 550 population.

The church was built in the 13th century and dedicated to St Lawrence. In the porch are the carved stone effigies of Sir Robert de Hilton and his lady. The churchyard is combined with the manor gardens and beautifully kept. In a field

The thriving hub of the village of Fulstow

near the church is a mound. This is said by some to be a mass grave for 118 villagers who died of 'the sweating sickness'. Another theory is that the graves contain cattle struck down by a plague.

Until 1969 there were two pubs in the village, the Lord Nelson and the Cross Keys, but only the latter remains. The post office and general store, still a thriving business, is a lively meeting place for villagers.

Farming is the main occupation in the village – predominantly cereals, potatoes and beef cattle, and there is also a large egg producing farm.

Not far away lives Mr P. Clark, a railway enthusiast who has a collection of steam trains that he has restored and which can often be seen steaming up and down the track laid on his land.

⌘ GEDNEY

In the Domesday Book Gedney was called Gadenai, taking its name from the enclosure of spikes which in Anglo-Saxon times was used to protect the island on which the church stands from roving bands coming into the Wash from the mainland of Europe. The sea in those times was so near that the island was surrounded at each high tide.

About the time of the Norman Conquest, Gedney had a Goose Fair – geese, sheep and donkeys were plentiful in the district. From the 12th century onwards large areas were drained, reclaimed and turned into rich arable land.

Seawards, beyond the last enclosure, the foreshore is now used by the Royal Air Force as a practice bombing range. In 1883 the Gedney Common Enclosure bank of 1874 gave way and the whole marsh was flooded to several feet. Before the advent of the car, Bank Holiday trips to the sea marsh by horse and wagon were popular; the great attractions being the roundabouts, swings and stalls selling mussels, cockles and samphire all collected off the marsh. Local people still gather the samphire which when cooked and pickled is eaten with cold meat.

The main feature of Gedney is certainly the church, a lovely stone building of Early English, Late Decorated and Perpendicular styles. It has an outstanding 14th century Jesse window which is similar to that in Chartres Cathedral in France.

In 1982 the village was visited by over 400 people whose surname was Gedney, Gadney or Gidney. They travelled from Canada, America, Australia and many parts of Great Britain to meet and take part in a special service in Gedney church. The postmaster had been given special dispensation for letters to be franked in Gedney.

⌘ GIPSEY BRIDGE

This nucleus of houses in the parish of Thornton le Fen is grouped where the road from Frithville carries the main traffic around Boston to Langrick. It is a

The Gipsey bridge

predominantly agricultural area with ribbon development housing on the Coningsby road.

Since the 1960s three new housing estates have been built to enlarge the village. In 1987 the once abandoned public house The Windmill was reopened. There is a shop-cum-post office and a county primary school. A Methodist chapel stands at the roadside and a few meetings are held in its school room.

No one has the real story about the name Gipsey, but the bridge over the stream, which is now the Castledyke Drain, gives its name to the village. One theory is that gipsey means 'wandering', so it is the 'bridge over the wandering stream'.

⌘ GOSBERTON

Six miles from Spalding, at the A16 and A152 road junction, the village is overlooked by the parish church of St Peter and St Paul. Viewed from any direction it is a pleasing sight. Certainly from the Boston and Eaudike roads at sundown one can see the tall steeple majestically rising from surrounding trees in sharp silhouette against a crimson sky – a fine example of the lovely sunsets the fenlands of Lincolnshire can be proud of.

The present spelling was established in the 1500s but in the Domesday Book both 'Gozeberdecca' and 'Gosberkirk' are recorded. It is a compact village from which straggling roads reach out to various hamlets embraced within the parish – Belnie, Westhorpe, Rigbolt, Cheal, Clough and Risegate. All are steeped in history with Saxon, Danish and Roman influences and indicative that Gosberton rose from the marshes.

Gosberton Bank is a reminder of the Romans' foresight to avoid encroachment by the sea. From here, on a clear day, as many as a dozen different churches can be counted. Nearby Risegate Eau, Hammond Beck and Forty Foot drains are evidence of the hard work involved to rid the area of waterlogging and achieve its present fertile state.

Springtime in Gosberton is indeed pleasant – many by-roads are planted with flowering bulbs and most gardens offer a colourful display. Visitors from near and far stop here for refreshment as they journey to see the bulbfields, Spalding Flower Parade and many decorated churches and chapels. Gosberton's three denominations all put tremendous effort into the lovely arrangements.

⌘ GOXHILL

In medieval times Goxhill grew as the village serving the adjacent port or 'haven' – now silted up. It retained its strategic importance until the paddle ferries operating from nearby New Holland were replaced by the new Humber Bridge.

It was here that an RAF bomber base was established in the Second World War. However, due to its proximity to Kingston upon Hull, too much Luftwaffe attention was attracted and the airfield became an American Air Force training base.

Like many of the buildings scattered around the village the colossal church of All Saints has a proud and prosperous feel. The chief treasure within its light and spacious interior is a 15th century wall painting of the Crucifixion in the south porch. Older than the church is Goxhill Hall, south-east of the village centre. Wrongly known as Goxhill Priory the tall stone manor was, in fact, built for domestic use in the 14th century. Now incorporated into a range of farm buildings, a spiral 'newel' stairway leads from the vaulted ground floor 'barn' to the main chamber above.

Older still is Thornton Abbey, two miles south of the village. Here the main glory is the towering fortified gatehouse, displaying a row of four octagonal stone turrets and a series of carved statues.

⌘ GREAT GONERBY

The village of Great Gonerby is one of the oldest in the Grantham area. The early settlement was a little out of the actual site of the village and there are remains of a Roman camp in the Ridge area.

The clock on the church in Great Gonerby was once the target for 'clock pelters'

Later camps were set up by Cromwell in the 17th century and he himself lodged in a house in Pond Street locally known as 'Cromwell's Cottage'. Here he must have planned his attack on Grantham, as the village stands 300 ft above the town.

The church stands on the site of an ancient Saxon place of worship and has an interesting stone alcove and other Tudor effigies and carvings. The clock has been the target of the 'clock pelters', who pelted the face with either stones or clods of earth to try to stop the clock so that no one knew the time and the workers would go home earlier – whether it really worked for or against them is difficult to know!

The hill down into Grantham has been lowered by ten to fifteen feet but it is still quite steep and when it was the Great North Road, which took all traffic through the village, one can imagine the difficulties of the stage coaches and the ease with which highwaymen were able to hold up and rob the travellers. There were teams of heavy horses to haul up the stage coaches and in inclement weather it was often impossible to make the journey through.

The houses in the Main Street are mostly Georgian, although several are much earlier, and built of Ancaster stone. In Green Street was a side road called The

Wong and this was used to gather the livestock before sending them to Grantham market. The name has been removed within the last few years and it is now part of Green Street.

⌘ GREAT PONTON

Great Ponton is a pleasant village largely nestled between the A1 and the waters of the Cringle brook and the river Witham. It is said to be the 'Ad Pontem' of the Romans. Ermine Street to the east of the village, numerous finds relating to the Roman period and the discovery of a mosaic pavement in a field to the north of the present school, bear testimony to the presence of those foreign invaders of long ago.

The church of the Holy Cross stands in an elevated position in the village. It is dominated by a splendid and lofty tower built in 1519 by Anthony Ellys, a wool merchant of the Staple of Calais who lived in his manor house adjacent to the church. It is a fine example of Perpendicular style. On the three outer faces is the legend 'Thynke and Thanke God of All'. The tower was Anthony Ellys's thank-offering for preservation and material success. Travelling abroad must have been

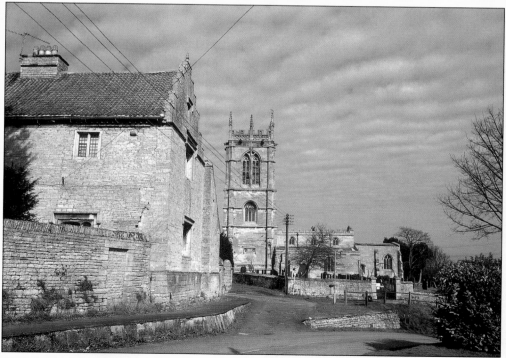

The lofty tower of Holy Cross church and the manor house, Great Ponton

dangerous in those days, particularly for someone carrying money, and one story tells of barrels of Calais sand being delivered to the manor house. Hidden in the sand was gold secreted there by the wool merchant!

The fiddle weather-vane on the church tower is believed to be unique in England. Legend has it that many years ago a fiddler used to visit Great Ponton to entertain the villagers. When he announced his intention of going to America the villagers paid his fare. In America he made his fortune and when he returned he had the weather-vane erected. The fiddle is attached to one of the eight crocketed pinnacles of the tower. It is said that it revolves on an old ginger-beer bottle marble. After it blew down in 1978 and had to be refixed, it was found to be weathered to the thinness of brown paper!

⌘ HAGWORTHINGHAM

Hagworthingham is a village with narrow twisting lanes, and is reached on the A158 (Skegness) road midway between Spilsby and Horncastle. It is sometimes called Hag, which is a pity because such a pretty place does not deserve an ugly name.

It is close to the site of the battle of Winceby (1643) and to Snipedales Nature Reserve and Country Park, developed by the Lincolnshire Trust for Nature Conservation.

The Old Hall on the Main Road is an 18th century house. The New Hall on the corner of Church Lane is a Georgian private residence, nicely restored and maintained.

Stockwith Mill was mentioned by Tennyson in his poem, *The Brook*. The buildings, which are 18th century, are used as a restaurant and craft shop.

There is evidence of 12th, 13th and 15th century work on Holy Trinity church and until the 1970s it had a peal of eight bells. Sadly the bells were sold to Welbourn (Lincoln) to raise money for the repair to the tower which collapsed in 1972. The churchyard overlooks a valley in the beautiful Wolds and a barrow believed to be a very old burial mound can be seen on the way to Lusby a mile away through the beck, which has a footbridge.

Hagworthingham windmill is a reminder of the milling and merchant business of the Ellis family. The village pump has been restored in Manor Road.

There are many attractions in this delightful area and Hagworthingham remains one of the unspoiled villages of the Wolds.

⌘ HECKINGTON

The village is recorded in the Domesday survey as Echintune and was then held by Gilbert de Gaunt. There was a church here in 1086, but the present St Andrew's church is at least the third building to stand on the same site and is considered to be one of the finest parish churches of the Decorated period.

Adjacent to Heckington station is the last surviving eight-sailed windmill in England. The mill was acquired by the County Council in 1953. After restoration it is now grinding again at weekends. The windmill is open to the public as is the nearby Craft and Heritage Centre, which is still known as the Pearoom because, before its restoration by Heckington Village Trust, the building was owned by a well-known seed firm and local people worked there sorting peas.

It is claimed that Dick Turpin slept at The Nag's Head, an inn near the village green. This may well be the case, as at his trial in York, Turpin was convicted of

The delightful beck runs through the centre of Heighington

stealing a mare and foal from Heckington common. After a second trial for stealing another horse from the same owner he was sentenced and executed a month later, on the 7th April 1739.

Samuel Jessup (born 1752), a wealthy grazier of Heckington, consumed 226,934 pills and drank 40,000 bottles of medicine over the years before he died at the age of 65!

In 1811 the first English aeronaut, Mr James Sadler, flew his hydrogen balloon at a record average speed of 84 mph in a gale between Birmingham and Heckington. Sadler fell out whilst attempting to land but his co-pilot Burcham continued until he encountered an ash tree.

⌘ HEIGHINGTON

Heighington lies four miles south-east of Lincoln. A beck runs from the Old Mill through the centre of the village where there are some fine stone houses. It has a unique chapel of ease with schoolroom adjoining, the tower being 13th century, and a Victorian Methodist chapel close by.

Heighington has been designated a Lincoln 'Main Village', and therefore boasts all the necessary amenities, including a modern primary school, two village halls and a sports field.

⌘ HEMSWELL

This is a quiet charming village, nestling at the foot of the limestone ridge, halfway between Lincoln and Scunthorpe. It was originally called Elmswell and was a part of the Aslacoe Wapentake.

Several interesting features are maintained. The chalybeate springs, once the main source of drinking water for the villagers (and which probably explain the name of the village) still run out of the hillside. Piped water came to the village in 1948. The pinfold, once a pound for stray cattle, was a small square of neglected ground until 1977 when the Parish Council had a stone wall built round it. A seat was installed and the Women's Institute and the Evergreen Club planted four shrubs there to commemorate the Queen's Silver Jubilee.

A maypole has been maintained here since the days when May Day was one of the highlights of the village calendar. Since it was refurbished in Jubilee year, 1977, maypole dancing has become an annual event once more. New braids were bought and costumes made for a team of twelve dancers. The boys' smocks are embroidered with the traditional patterns and the girls wear long petticoats and skirts and fen bridle style bonnets. It has become almost a tradition for the Lincoln Morris Men to attend this May Day Bank Holiday celebration, when everyone has the opportunity to dance around the maypole.

Hemswell's 'twin' village, Harpswell, is just the distance of a field away and is mainly a farming community spread beside the main road to the coast, the A631. It is overlooked by St Chad's church, which is proudly maintained by the small community and shares a vicar with Hemswell and Glentworth.

⌘ HOLDINGHAM

One mile to the north of Sleaford is the hamlet of Holdingham (formerly spelled Haldingham). Holdingham is noted for being the presumed birthplace of Richard-de-Haldingham. Originally a cleric in the diocese of Lincoln, he was made a Canon of Hereford in 1299. While there he produced the 'Mappa Mundi'. Now in Hereford Cathedral, this is one of the earliest maps in England. It represents the world as an island, surrounded by ocean, with Jerusalem as its centre.

The Jolly Scotchman public house was redecorated by the brewery in the mid 1950s. Not realising the name had nothing to do with Scotland, they used Scotch plaid in the interior and men were represented doing the Highland Fling and playing the bagpipes in the two main stained glass windows. In fact it stands on the site of the old toll gatehouse and was so named after the keeper who used to 'scotch' the wheels of the carts while the owners went to pay their toll. The public house sign was altered some years ago and now shows the 'Jolly Scotchman'.

⌘ HOLTON BECKERING

Holton Beckering lies in pleasant countryside some twelve miles north-east of Lincoln and about three miles north of the main road from Lincoln to Skegness.

In Beckering (which in much earlier days was separate from, and more populous than, Holton) can still be seen some bumps and hollows in the ground that indicate a deserted medieval village. People digging in their gardens occasionally turn up pieces of old pottery or old clay pipes. Deep ploughing has destroyed most of the 'ridge and furrow' which was visible in many of the fields, although they can be seen and photographed from the air.

The church of All Saints, built some five or six centuries ago, is a handsome building which in spite of restoration still has some original features. There are the two large shields carved on the stone wall on either side of the south porch, with the arms of Roos and de Bekering. The beautiful reredos was made at the time of lavish restoration in the second half of the 19th century by an Italian craftsman who was an expert in gold mosaic work. The motifs of angels playing musical instruments are particularly interesting.

The Holton estate was sold in 1917, and the Hall was occupied by a succession of owners, until it was taken over by the Army as a convalescent home. In 1945 it was bought by a community of pacifists to house conscientious objectors who had been given land work as an alternative to military service. A few of them with their descendants still live in the village. The Hall is now in private ownership, but the 'big room' is used by the village for meetings, harvest suppers and the like.

⌘ HOLTON LE MOOR

To see England at its best, the England that romantic poets write about, visit Holton le Moor on a spring morning and take a walk down Gatehouse Lane, where fresh green leaves make a tunnel over one's head. Near a bend is the Woodman's white cottage, with its neat box-edged path and blossoming apple tree.

On the opposite side of the road is a glimpse of the Park, with cattle grazing under the trees and a red brick Georgian house, which has been the home of the Dixon-Gibbons family since the 1780s. At one time the entire village was owned by the family. The houses they built have the unusual feature of name plaques. These names make an interesting study giving clues to the history of the village.

At the same time it is possible to note various types of brickwork and bricks used in the construction and ornamentation of the houses. Pargetting decorates many buildings and shows the history of Britain as well as of the village.

Some pargetting appears on the nearby school including a list of names of the first pupils to be taught there. The school, with its colourful plaque of 'For God, King and Country' over its doors, is set in spacious playgrounds, including the March Yard. This pleasant, secluded area is open for public use and earned its name from the fact that the militia were trained there by the then High Sheriff.

Adjoining this is St Luke's churchyard, with its wide variety of plant life and different species of birds. The church has a turret which contains two bells, made from the original bell given by Nicholas Bestoe. This was broken when the tower was destroyed, but a rubbing was taken of the inscription, which is in the church.

Built in 1910 the Moot Hall is an interesting and attractive building. The iron railings outside bear the slogan 'Holton will flourish if all do their share.'

⌘ HORKSTOW

Horkstow is one of a string of villages sheltering below the steep western escarpment of the Lincolnshire Wolds. There is open access to roam among the lovely tree-dotted pastures rising behind the village, from where magnificent views open up over Horkstow's handsome red-brick buildings and the whole of the Ancholme valley beyond. Even the chancel of Saint Maurice's church is brick built, although the rest of the church is stone. Inside the church the chancel appears as a raised cavern, reached by ten steps, which is due to the 17th century addition of the Shirley family vault beneath it.

Horkstow Hall is built on the site of what must have been a sizeable Roman villa. Three substantial sections of a Roman mosaic pavement were discovered here in 1796, portraying a chariot race and Orpheus taming the wild beast. From

The village of Horkstow

the Hall a narrow lane leads down to the river Ancholme, here spanned by a unique suspension bridge, designed by Sir John Rennie in the 1840s. It is supported by rustic stone arches and neatly painted in red and green.

Perhaps Horkstow's most noted resident was George Stubbs, who commenced his gruesome horse dissections for his book *Anatomy of the Horse* here in 1746 – several local families own examples of his work, from his stay in the village.

⌘ HUTTOFT

Huttoft, a very pleasant village on the East Coast, of Danish origin, lies between the villages of Mumby and Sutton-on-Sea. The population is approximately 480.

Access to the beach at Huttoft Bank is about three miles away, and can be reached via Jolly Common Lane or Sea Lane. Car parking, picnicking and caravanning facilities are to be found in this area.

The church of St Margaret dates back to the early 13th century, and the county primary school nearby was built in 1840. The Methodist chapel dates back to 1857. Services are held regularly at both places of worship. Other amenities to be found in the village are a petrol station and garage, a post office, shop, animal feeds mill, village hall and public house.

Ingham's spacious and picturesque village green

Activities in the village over the years have included a playgroup, Mothers and Toddlers group, Over 50s club, Bingo, Youth Club and Women's Institute (founded in 1922).

There are numerous public footpaths in the area for those who enjoy walking in these beautiful surroundings.

⌘ INGHAM

Ingham nestles at the foot of the Lincoln Edge, eight miles north of Lincoln. There has been a settlement here since the time of the Saxons and Danes, as the ending of the name 'ham' indicates. In the Domesday Book, it is spelled Ingeham.

In the centre of the village is a spacious, picturesque, tree scattered village green. The village originally grew up around the green, a cluster of grey stone houses and cottages, added to later by the Victorians.

There has been a church here since the 13th century, but the present church of All Saints was rebuilt about 1796, reportedly after a fire. In front of the churchyard is a second small village green, until about 35 years ago the village pond, but now a tree-shaded oasis of peace, with a seat for quiet reflection.

The village is only three miles from Scampton RAF camp, where the Red Arrows are based, and from October to February we enjoy thrilling free shows as they rehearse their routines.

For the walker, there are a number of easy and interesting walks in the vicinity of the village, with a number of public footpaths. The Black Horse, built 300 years ago, is situated on the edge of the green and maintains its old world charm. The Black Horse is a typical cosy village pub renowned as being a haunt of the Dambusters during the Second World War.

⌘ KEELBY

Saxons, Romans and Normans all passed this way, Keelby being mentioned in the Domesday Book as Chelebi. The name, meaning 'ridge village', was given by the Danes.

The oldest buildings are a tiny medieval domestic chapel, incorporated into Church Farm house, and the medieval church of St Bartholomew. An interesting memorial is to two sisters, Annie and Dorothy Lancaster, victims of the *Titanic* disaster.

The old part of Keelby, lying near the church and playing field, is quite distinct. Here, there is a short row of five old cottages whose thick chalk walls have been raised in brick and re-roofed.

To make life easier for those who are unwell or getting on in years, there are modern council bungalows, sheltered flats at Hubert Ward House, named after a popular village doctor, and a residential home at Walnut House, this same doctor's old home. Among several bequests, one by Mrs Alice South in 1605 still provides a small gift at Christmas for several retired villagers.

Walking is easy, with access to Brocklesby, the Earl of Yarborough's estate village, Limber with its mausoleum, Roxton Woods, the springs which flow into Suddle Beck babbling gaily after a rainstorm, and several bridle paths; horse riding is a popular activity here.

A great beauty of this district is its wide open vistas, the vast skies and glorious sunsets. If you come to Keelby, take a walk down little Topper Lane, which is the truly country bit of the village. In winter, admire the snowdrops and aconites nearby and in spring, the beautiful pink and white cherry trees in Manor Street. For those who know where to look, it is easy to find wild flowers, foliage and even bay for flavouring the cooking.

⌘ KETTLETHORPE & TORKSEY

The hamlets of Kettlethorpe, Laughterton and Fenton are situated eleven miles

Torksey village

north-west of Lincoln with the Roman Foss Dyke and the river Trent on their borders.

Kettlethorpe is famous for its connection with Lady Katherine Swynford, third wife of John of Gaunt, Duke of Lancaster, an ancestress of our present Royal Family by the Beaufort line. All that remains of her home, the property of her first husband Sir Hugh Swynford, is the old archway and part of the moat.

Laughterton is on the A1133 and has caravan sites, a scout camp and a golf course. There is easy access to the river Trent via Marsh Lane and the area is very popular with anglers. The local inn is called The Friendship.

Fenton, the other corner of the triangle of villages, has an old maltings and the local inn, The Carpenter's Arms.

Torksey has many attractions. It is a village for boating (at Torksey Lock), fishing and golf, but has a past much more important that its size suggests today. It is mentioned in the Domesday Book as a town, and before that was a focal point for the Roman defences, where the Foss Dyke joins the Trent. Torksey Lock has a pleasant river bank walk. Pottery was found when the site known as Little London was excavated and it is known there were thriving potteries in the area. Torksey pottery can be seen at the Usher Gallery in Lincoln. The village has a well-sited ruin known as Torksey Castle, built in the 16th century. It was sacked by the Royalists to rout the Cromwellians during the Civil War and was never rebuilt.

⌘ KIRKBY-CUM-OSGODBY

The administrative parish of Kirkby-cum-Osgodby is made up of four villages – Kirkby, Osgodby, Kingerby and Usselby.

Kingerby, once a larger community, is now a sparsely populated area reaching down to the river Ancholme at its western boundary. St Peter's church (13th century), now in the care of the Redundant Churches Fund, is, possibly, the third church on the site of what was once a Roman camp.

South of the church, on a great circular mound, stands a 19th century hall. This is an ancient site which has yielded pre-Roman skeletons and artefacts believed to be of the New Stone Age.

Moving eastwards we come to the neat and compact village of Kirkby with the church dedicated to St Andrew. The oldest work, tower and chancel, dates from the 13th century but the nave was rebuilt in 1790. In the chancel is a rare double piscina. The chancel stands at a slight angle to the nave and the east window is also asymmetrical.

Osgodby (Osgotebi in the Domesday Book) is a long, straggling village to the south of Kingerby Beck. Buildings of note include the Methodist chapel of 1897 in red brick and a row of cottages of about 1840 built of locally handmade brick by a speculative builder, Nash, of Market Rasen.

On the eastern boundary of the parish lies the hamlet of Usselby. Here, at the end of a narrow lane from the main road (A46), stands St Margaret's church. This small building contains some medieval masonry but was remodelled in the 18th and 19th centuries. A nearby Georgian hall was, in the 1830s, in the possession of the Right Hon C. Tennyson d'Eyncourt, the uncle of Alfred Lord Tennyson the poet laureate.

⌘ KIRTON IN HOLLAND

The fact that Kirton in Holland has a town hall, a town football club and a town brass band, indicates immediately that it is a large village, though no longer the third largest settlement in Lincolnshire, as it was in the reign of Elizabeth I. Situated four miles south of Boston, Kirton is a busy, bustling village with its wide main street fringed with a useful variety of shops, and other offices of modern life. It is surrounded by areas of marshland which introduce a sense of desolation and timelessness. Mentioned in the Domesday Book and long identified in various forms of the word 'Chircetune', Kirton's early development owed much to attempts at draining the area by successive invaders and then to the taming of its inhabitants by the Normans.

Until the mid 17th century livestock dominated local farming but the Enclosures Act saw changes which so incensed those who kept geese on the marshes that rioting took place, men were killed, animals poisoned and farm

The wide tree-lined main street in Kirton in Holland

buildings fired. Nowadays, the marshes are much enjoyed by wildfowlers and naturalists, and lush samphire is still collected for boiling or pickling.

Formed in 1870 and one of the oldest in the country, Kirton Town Brass Band has played at all major events including fetes and festivals, sports days, coronations and jubilees. The band played while 1,600 sat down to tea on the village green to mark Queen Victoria's Jubilee in 1897 and in the 1960s its prowess was such that it reached the final stages of national competition in London.

⌘ LAUGHTON

Laughton lies about three quarters of a mile to the west of the A159 road which links Gainsborough and Scunthorpe in the fertile Vale of Trent. Close by is Laughton Forest, a vast area of woodland which is mainly coniferous but with attractive belts of deciduous trees. Laughton Wood, which is close to the A159, was first planted between 1783 and 1789. Access to the forest is limited but an area to the north is open to the public and there are many pleasant walks.

The village itself consists of old red brick farms and cottages interspersed with modern houses and bungalows clustered around the church. Although of medieval origin, All Saints' church was extensively and elaborately restored in 1896 by the eminent Victorian architect G. F. Bodley. The restoration work was made possible by the generosity of the Hon Mrs Meynell-Ingram in memory of her late husband, Hugo; the Meynell-Ingram family's connection with Laughton can be traced back to the time of Elizabeth I.

Across the road from the church is an interesting grouping of school, school house and reading room. The latter now serves as a village meeting place. The school itself flourishes and has long outgrown the original building dated 1841. Laughton Endowed School is notable as it was founded as a grammar school in 1566 and has continued in constant use since that time.

Originally a carpenter's shop, the Ingram Arms was opened in 1975. Although there was a public house in the vicinity in the 19th century, it was closed over a hundred years ago on the orders of the lady of the manor who felt it encouraged licentiousness amongst the villagers!

⌘ LEADENHAM

Leadenham village lies on the Lincolnshire Cliff, almost midway between Lincoln and Grantham. It was mentioned in the Domesday survey of 1086, when it already had its own church. The building of the present church began in about 1320.

In the 14th century a manor and a small plot of land were given to the prioress and nuns of the Abbey of Heveninges. In 1377 a small group of nuns was sent to Leadenham to live in the manor and to establish a hospice. Pilgrims on their way to visit the shrine of St Hugh at Lincoln would have been thankful to find a safe resting place for the night and to share meals prepared by the nuns from produce grown on their plot of land. This enclosure adjoining the present village hall is still known as Nun's Close.

At this time the wool trade was growing rapidly and wealthy merchants would travel through Leadenham with fleeces to sell in Lincoln. They too would stop at the hospice. They could afford to be generous and the church of St Swithun in Leadenham owes much to their generosity and patronage.

A railway line used to run through Leadenham, until it was closed in the 1960s. As there was a long siding at Leadenham station, Queen Victoria's train used to stop here overnight on her way to Scotland. In the Second World War the Royal Train stopped here when members of the Royal Family were visiting nearby RAF stations such as Scampton and Waddington.

The Reeve family have lived at Leadenham House since 1738 and still own much of the surrounding land. Leadenham is one of the few remaining estate villages in the county. The squire has always been patron of the church and has not only appointed the rector, but has, down the ages, encouraged the villagers to care for and support the church.

⌘ LEGBOURNE

The village of Legbourne is situated on the edge of the Lincolnshire Wolds some three and a half miles south-east of the market town of Louth, on the A157 road, and is within easy reach of the East Coast resort of Mablethorpe.

The Cistercian priory was founded by Robert Fitz Gilbert de Lekeburn in the 12th century. It was occupied by nuns and when it was finally dissolved in the reign of Henry VIII, it is recorded that it had a yearly income of £38.8s.4d. The site of the priory is in the grounds of Legbourne Abbey, at present a private house.

The village pump, an imposing canopied and pinnacled stone structure standing in front of the church, was built by Canon J. Overton in 1877 in memory of his mother. The pump was the principal supply of water to the village until 1953.

Before the infamous Beeching cuts the East Lincolnshire section of the Great Northern Railway, built in 1863, ran to the west of the village. Legbourne station was just outside the village and the old station house, now a private residence, can be seen on the right just before entering the village. The platform and a new building, constructed in the form of an engine shed, housed a most interesting railway museum but sadly it closed a few years ago.

A Legbourne man, Alfred Smith, gave his life to pioneer work on the use of X rays. He eventually suffered from the effects of radiation and from 1913 onwards his life was one of intense suffering, having had one leg amputated and being half blind. Having exhausted his savings he was compelled to sell his home and was granted a small pension by the Carnegie Hero Fund which enabled him to come to Legbourne to live in an old army hut, where he took up poultry farming to support his family. He died in 1933 and was buried in Grimsby.

⌘ LONG BENNINGTON

Long Bennington lies between Newark and Grantham on the Lincolnshire/Nottinghamshire border. Archaeological excavations have revealed a Bronze Age burial ground and the sites of Roman villas.

The Cistercian Order built a priory here in 1150, and there were monks at Bennington until 1642. Nothing remains of the actual structure of the priory, but the sites of the fish ponds can still be seen.

The church was built before 1086, for the Domesday Book recorded 'a church with a priest'. Today St Swithun's is an amalgam of styles from the 12th to 19th centuries, with the little that remains of the earlier church incorporated in its south doorway.

In the latter half of the 19th century a plan, approved by the Bishop, to rebuild the church in the centre of the village was put to all the householders. The response was favourable, but alas the £5,000 needed to carry out the work could not be raised. And so the church still stands where it always did; in a pleasant, open position, being almost the last house at the Grantham end of the village.

But there was to be a church in the centre of the village after all, for after a disagreement with the vicar in 1890 the lady of the manor had one built, at a cost of £650. She also at her own expense provided a curate who took the services.

The Crown public house in Maltby was once three small cottages

Long Bennington must always have been a lively village, standing as it did on the old medieval route from London to York. Never more so than in the Civil War, when it had Royalist Newark on one hand and Parliamentarian Grantham on the other. Its inhabitants would be used to the sight of horses and carriages passing through, or stopping at one of the coaching inns, the White Lion maybe.

⌘ MALTBY-LE-MARSH

The village of Maltby-le-Marsh is situated on the A1104, two miles west of Mablethorpe and five miles north of Alford.

The church of All Saints is mentioned in the Domesday Book, though it has been rebuilt at least three times. The tower is about 250 years old, and the chancel 200 years old, but the nave is very much older.

There were three schools at one time in Maltby, long before Mablethorpe had even one. In 1705 Mrs Anne Bolle 'gave and devised a farm' to pay for a schoolmaster to teach poor children their catechism. The Anne Bolle charity is still used to provide money for educational purposes for village children, and '40 shillings' is still distributed to the elderly at Christmas.

The Methodist church stands near the village centre, and was built in 1873 to replace the Wesleyan chapel which was immediately opposite. This is now a private dwelling, 'The Chantry'. A school room at the rear is used by many organisations, as it is the only room in the village available for public use.

There were two public houses in Maltby. The Crown still thrives and was once three small cottages and until the late 1940s the western boundary of the car park was the site of the village smithy. The other pub used to be the Turk's Head, another old building of interest, which was built in the 18th century. It was reputed to be haunted by the ghost of a First World War soldier.

In the heart of the village is the shop, built in 1780. There have been many additions over the years, and in 1909 it was granted a post office licence, still current. Opposite is a private printing works.

The windmill, built in the 1840s, was working until the 1950s. It also included a bakery. These buildings are now the Old Mill Restaurant, which also offers accommodation.

Willow Farm Caravan Park has grown from two caravans in the 1950s to having over 100 on site 50 years later.

⌘ MARSHCHAPEL

Marshchapel was once part of the parish of Fulstow. As the sea receded and more people found a living at the east end of the parish, a chapel was built. The first written evidence of this was in 1387, when the rector of Fulstow was directed to find a vicar for 'The Chapel in the Marsh'.

The western boundary separating the two parishes was drawn on an old watercourse, which is now roughly the route of the old Louth Navigation Canal. The southern boundary follows a pre-Roman track known as The Salters Way. Salt was the chief industry from pre-Roman times until the 16th century, evidence of which abounds on the eastern side of the ancient sea bank, shown as undulations in the fields. There is still evidence of medieval strip farming in the grass fields near the church; it was enclosed in 1841.

The early 15th century Perpendicular church is dedicated to St Mary. The treble bell, recast in 1919, bears the names of the eight men of the parish who died in the First World War.

The Old Hall at Marshchapel was built in 1720, during the reign of George I. The first owners were the Loft family. Mary Loft, who died in the late 1700s, had 19 children, all of whom died during infancy – the sad row of little graves can be seen in Marshchapel churchyard.

The restored Methodist chapel on the main street also serves as a community centre. Inside is a plaque commemorating an earlier chapel of 1795.

A windmill stands on the east of the main road. It was originally a post mill, erected by Charles Ryland before 1595 on a site gifted to him by the Monarch.

Martin Dales is popular with fisher folk

The mill served the neighbouring villages and remained working until 1837, when it was replaced by the present mill, erected by George Bull Bros of Hull, to the order of the Addiscombe family of Grimsby.

⌘ MARTIN DALES

The area of Martin Dales can be defined by the river Witham on its eastern boundary, Blankney Dales to the north, Walcott Dales to the south, and merging into Martin Fen and Timberland Fen to the west.

If there has to be a centre to Martin Dales one could say Kirkstead, as it is popular with the locals and many hundreds who come to fish from the river bank between June and March every year. There is also a large car park and it is the headquarters of the Angling Clubs Association.

In Church Road one will find St Hugh's church hall. This hall started life as a garage, which was bought and turned into a church hall to replace the old church when it was pulled down, because of its poor state of repair. The money to buy the hall had been raised by the people of the Dales, by sheer hard work and determination to have their own place of worship once again. The church hall is part of the Trinity church, Martin. The Waterside Methodist chapel is on the roadway which runs alongside the river and is still in use today with a very active Sunday school.

Kirkstead Bridge spans the river Witham. This bridge was built to replace the old railway bridge, which in its day had to be swung open to allow river traffic to pass through, causing traffic holdups on either side. The railway station has been closed for many years.

Martin Dales is a very rural area. The main occupation is naturally agriculture and is mainly arable, growing cereals, sugar beet, potatoes, beans for stock feed, and oil rape seed giving a beautiful yellow carpet of flowers from May to July. There are a number of small farms owned by the Lincolnshire County Council and rented by tenants, and larger privately owned farms.

⌘ MARTON

Marton has seen much history in the making for it lies where the Roman legions would have crossed the Trent. The ford they used, dating back to Hadrian's time, can still be seen in periods of severe drought.

The river used to be quite busy with tugs towing strings of barges to Lincoln or Boston, but the pleasure boat is the sight nowadays. The Egre, or tidal bore, reaches as far as Marton and beyond and to see a high one is quite an experience. There is a signposted footpath via the cliff top. Following this path gives a lovely view of the river meandering through the marshes.

Prominent also are the power stations, standing on the Nottingham side of the river, which are responsible for this area being dubbed 'Megawatt Valley'. Almost at the end of the clifftop path stands a windmill, built in 1799 but largely dismantled in 1926. A corn warehouse, a malthouse and a wharf to serve them also stood here when it was a port, hence the name Trentport.

Almost in the centre of the village stands the church of St Margaret of Antioch. Much of the work of both Normans and Saxons is retained. Its tall unbuttressed tapering tower was built in the 11th century. It has walls entirely of fine herringbone work right up to the bellchamber. The tall cross in the churchyard, restored and used as a war memorial, is thought to have been an old market butter cross.

A Lincolnshire directory published in 1876 names the keepers of three public houses in Marton, but of these only one remains today, the Ingleby Arms with its pleasant gardens and play area.

The large house at the bottom of the hill where Tillbridge Lane runs down into the village was known as the Black Swan and was a coaching inn until 1860. Dick Turpin is reputed to have spent the night here on his way to York.

⌘ MORTON (NR BOURNE)

Morton is a large village of brick and stone on the very edge of the fens. The long village street lined with attractive houses leads up to the west front of the church, dedicated to St John the Baptist. The church dominates the east of the village and resembles a miniature cathedral. The little priest's door in the south wall of the chancel belonged to an earlier church and may be late 12th century. Crossing the A15 the newer part of the village to the west is overlooked by richly wooded uplands.

In the 1880s there were at least 17 farmers in Morton and Hanthorpe. Many of them had other trades. Daniel Baker doubled as a blacksmith, William Hall was both farmer and coal merchant and William Clark was a farmer, butcher and landlord of the Five Bells. Samuel Eayes was grocer, baker and draper; Richard Steel, chemist and druggist and grocer; Williamson Bros were grocers, bakers and corn millers. The record for multiple jobs was held by Jesse Stow, who was schoolmaster, rate collector, vestry clerk, land measurer, organist and insurance agent!

The Sunday after 6th July is known as Feast Sunday. Until recent years it was the custom on that day for the children of the village to parade from the old school to the church, preceded by the village band. They brought gifts of eggs and flowers for distribution to the hospitals of the district. Although there is no parade or band now, the children still bring their gifts to the Feast Day Service.

⌘ NAVENBY

One of the string of villages along the A607 Lincoln to Grantham road, Navenby stands high on the Cliff, with excellent views down into the Brant valley.

The main High Street is a pleasant conservation area with listed buildings of stone, many of which have been restored in recent years. To the east of the village runs Ermine Street, which was the pilgrims' way from York to Canterbury. Around this area relics and coins from the Roman era have been found, which suggests that a Roman settlement may have been the beginning of this community.

As long ago as 1221 Navenby was granted a charter to hold a fair and markets, and in recent years a carnival was organised to revive this right. Agriculture has always played an important part in the area, especially in the Middle Ages, when the village had a weekly market around the butter cross on the village green.

At the beginning of the century there were six public houses, but today there are only three, one of which is the Lion & Royal Hotel which has the Prince of Wales feathers displayed over the front door. This was presented by Edward VII, Prince of Wales, when he stopped to change his clothes after hunting in 1870. A brass plate bearing the inscription 'In this room HRH Prince of Wales changed his clothes' can be seen in one of the bedrooms!

As early as 1857 Navenby had its own gas works, but all that remains today is the name of the lane. The church of St Peter is chiefly 14th century, but the north-west pillar of the five nave arcades (more massive than the rest) has stood since about 1180. On the north side of the sanctuary is the Easter Sepulchre, being one

A tranquil spot in the bustling village of Nettleham

of two within the county of Lincolnshire. The western tower has six bells, which are still rung for services today.

⌘ NETTLEHAM

Nettleham lies three miles north of Lincoln. The centre of the village is designated as a conservation area. There is visual evidence of Nettleham's long history alongside the Methodist chapel, where large grassy mounds mark the site of the 11th century Bishop's Palace, an ancient monument of national importance and yet to be fully explored.

The traditional green forms a focal point in the village, with many stone cottages around the green and on the High Street dating from the 16th, 17th, 18th and 19th centuries. The street around the green bustles with activity as this accommodates most of the shops and also leads to the health centre and public library.

The parish church, a listed building rebuilt in 1891, exhibits work of the 13th, 14th and 15th centuries. It stands in a pleasant setting of trees and by its side is a quiet, natural area with seats and footpaths. It is approached from the High Street by way of a footbridge over the beck which flows through the village. The beck runs alongside the road in the vicinity of the church and then a footpath provides a pleasant waterside walk. There are many attractive public 'right of way' walks and a plan of these is to be found in the library.

The village boasts a very large sports complex named after its twinned French village, Mulsanne. The children too have a playing field.

The Lincolnshire Police Headquarters has been built on the outskirts of Nettleham, adjacent to the A46 road.

Nettleham has assumed a dormitory function for Lincoln and many of the 3,200 residents work in the city. Property is very much sought after and Nettleham is considered to be one of the best villages in which to live.

⌘ NORMANBY LE WOLD

This small enclosed village lies near the highest point of the Lincolnshire Wolds, some 543 ft above sea level.

The church was largely restored in the Victorian era, but the tower is around 700 years old and the arches of the nave are 13th century. There is a curious corbel on the arch spanning the old south aisle, a carving of a man apparently in the throes of toothache, one hand raised to his head, the other holding his mouth wide open. There is also a fine medieval font like a pillar, enriched with a double band of quatrefoils and wavy pattern.

The church at the north-east is sheltered by some fine old beech and chestnut trees but the south side is exposed to the wind and rain from the prevailing south-west winds, and looks over the intervening valley to Walesby and the old church on the neighbouring hill.

In recent years a walk, part of the Viking Way, has become popular and its route passes within a few feet of the church tower, leading across fields at the top of the cliff and then steeply descending to the village of Walesby. The road into the village from Nettleton top commands magnificent views across the great Lincoln plain to the towers of Lincoln Cathedral and castle, and on a fine day the cooling towers of the Trent valley can be clearly seen.

⌘ NORTH KELSEY

North Kelsey has a long history and is mentioned in the Domesday Book of 1086, when it was called Norchelsie.

The main High Street zigzags its way through the village with a myriad assortment of little winding roads leading off it. In the centre of the village there is a triangular village green with a recently restored pump to one side. This is known as the Bywell. There is a story that the water has magical powers and whoever drinks it has no desire to leave the village.

The recently restored pump can be seen on North Kelsey's village green

All Hallows' church is built of local stone, a gingery brown in colour, very worn and weathered with a small squat square Norman tower. Two buildings of note are next to the church, the manor house and Church Farm. The manor house is built in traditional style and Church Farm is a striking black and white building.

The village has an extensive historical and archaeological background. There are strong links to Roman times, two sites of Roman villas are known in the village. Much information can be gained from the Rev A. Kerswill's book *North Kelsey, a brief history*.

Most of the village was owned by the Nelthorpe family of Scawby but in 1867 there was a great auction in Brigg, when much of the property was sold. If you look carefully round the village you can trace a particular style of brick decoration on some of the older houses which is also to be seen on some of the houses in Scawby.

The village sports club includes a tennis club and a bowls club. There is a sandpit next to the bowling green, the sand being of very fine quality and used for specialist work. In the sandpit there is a trace of a coral reef, left from the time aeons ago when North Kelsey was a coral island! This was in the time when there was a stagnant inland sea at nearby Greetwell.

⌘ NORTH SOMERCOTES

The village got its name from the reclaimed land on the coast originally called salt pans, which was turned into good grazing land. During the summer farmers from the Wolds brought their sheep down to graze, hence the name 'summer cots', being an old word for fields.

During the Second World War the RAF established a camp at Donna Nook, part of the village which borders the coastline and which was later used as a prisoner of war camp. This site is still used as a bombing range for planes from many parts of the world.

Along this part of the coast was a pack horse trail, starting at Tetney Haven and with a stop for refreshment at the old pub The Ark, which was nearly on the sea bank. For many years the lifeboat was launched at Donna Nook manned by a local crew. The coastguards still have a lookout on top of the dunes.

It is understood that this village was a favourite haunt for smugglers. The road known as Warren Road was the original sea bank. On this road is Locksley Hall which has an association with Tennyson. The village is well served with amenities, including many shops, garages, pubs, a Methodist church and the parish church of St Mary, which dates from the 13th century.

A holiday camp built on the former gravel pit is a venue for many hundreds of visitors during the summer. This is bordered on all sides by a forest of trees.

The village has one of the best playing fields in the area, providing for bowls, tennis, football and cricket. The money for the upkeep chiefly comes from the annual carnival.

⌘ OLD BOLINGBROKE

Lying in a dip of the Wolds, Old Bolingbroke is one of the most peaceful villages in Lincolnshire. Far from any main road, its present air of quiet calm must be very different from the days when it was an important market.

The reason for its medieval prosperity is indicated by the grassy foundations of Bolingbroke Castle, lying on the outskirts of the village. Built about 1220, it passed via various marriages into the hands of the House of Lancaster, and thus to the famous John of Gaunt, fourth son of Edward III and brother of the Black Prince. After his brother's death John of Gaunt became Regent of England on behalf of his young nephew – the ill-fated Richard II. In Bolingbroke Castle was born John's son, Henry of Bolingbroke, who later took the throne from his cousin Richard, and became Henry IV.

The castle eventually ceased to be a residence, and became an administrative centre for the Duchy of Lancaster and then gradually began to decay, probably because no one of enough importance lived in it to justify extensive repairs. But it was during the Civil War that the castle finally became 'one of the ruins that Cromwell knocked about a bit'. Bolingbroke was a Royalist stronghold and in 1643 it held out against a siege by Parliamentary troops from Horncastle until the Royalists were defeated at the nearby battle of Winceby. Subsequently the castle

Bolingbroke Castle was 'knocked about' by Oliver Cromwell

was systematically demolished by order of the Parliamentary authorities and much of the stone was removed by the villagers to build their own houses.

The village church of St Peter and St Paul was unluckily sited too near the castle for its own good. Built about 1363 it was originally three times its present size, but during the siege and attack on the castle in 1643 the church was so badly damaged that only the south aisle remained. After the Restoration of the Monarchy this aisle and what was left of the tower were patched up to make a serviceable village church with rather odd proportions.

⌘ OSBOURNBY

Osbournby, or Osberneby as it was recorded in the Domesday Book, is a small village on the A15, six miles south of Sleaford.

The manor once belonged to the Hussey family. In 1486 John Hussey fought in the battle of Stoke on the side of Henry VII and in 1509 was given large tracts of land in Lincolnshire. In 1537, having been accused and found guilty of taking part in a rebellion in Lincolnshire, he was executed at Tyburn. The Carr family bought the estate from the Husseys, and they brought sheep farming to the area from

Northumberland. In 1604 they founded the Carr's grammar school in Sleaford, still used today. After the Carrs, the Herveys took over and then the Whichcote family. The first Baron Whichcote was created in 1660 but when the eighth Baron died in 1949 the estate passed to Nicholas Plain, his nephew, who still owns Osbournby Hall, five farms and some cottages in the village.

The pub, the Whichcote Arms, takes its name from the local family and is situated on the main road, as is the village hall.

The parish church of St Peter and St Paul is a large building dating from the reign of Edward III. It still retains many of the old pew ends, which are richly carved. The font is Norman, ornamented with pillars and arches. There is also a Methodist church in the village, dating from 1874.

St Mary's church and the war memorial, Pinchbeck

⌘ PINCHBECK

The word 'pinchbeck' in English dictionaries means a copper and zinc alloy used in cheap jewellery, which was introduced by Christopher Pinchbeck, a London watchmaker who originated from this village. Pinchbeck is situated two miles from Spalding on the busy A16.

Records of the settlement go back hundreds of years and there was probably a wooden Saxon church in existence before the Norman Conquest. There is evidence that a Norman church was built about 1070 on the present site of St Mary's parish church and later an Early English church was erected on the Norman foundations. The present chancel and chapel were built about 1350, the tower and south porch being added later. Opposite the church stands a fine war memorial set in a tree-lined lawn.

At the other end of the village is the Baptist church. The first Baptist meeting place was established about 1840 and at one time Baptists were baptised in the river Glen, attracting crowds of spectators. The main village street is Knight Street, so named because of honours conferred upon the local Ogle family.

At one time annual horse races were held in the village on the Sunday nearest 22nd June, but apparently the event developed into a rather rowdy affair and finally ceased about 1850. These days the Pinchbeck Carnival is held in June.

During the Spalding Tulip Parade week, Pinchbeck church holds its own flower festival in company with other local churches. During this period the church tower is open and from the top a wonderful bird's eye view of the area can be obtained.

⌘ RAUCEBY

At the point where the Ancaster gap emerges into the fen areas around Sleaford lies the parish of North and South Rauceby, a mile apart, but sharing church, school, village hall and public house, with Rauceby Hall between.

The Boon beck, which forms the boundary between the villages, feeds the lake in the Hall grounds. In 1791 the land was enclosed. North Rauceby was very largely owned by the Earl of Bristol, an absentee landlord, but there were 14 owners in South Rauceby.

In 1842, Adlard Welby Esq of Parhamdam in South Rauceby sold his entire estate to Anthony Peacock, who extended his holding in the village so that it became an estate village. He built, on the site of Parhamdam, an imposing residence, Rauceby Hall, designed by the architect William Burn. He created the lake and planted many trees. Mr Peacock, who changed his name later to Willson, rebuilt many of the cottages in the village, but there are a number still surviving which were built in the 17th and 18th centuries, all of stone and red pantiled roofs.

The church, mentioned in the Domesday Book, is dedicated to St Peter and has a tower and a broach spire of the 13th century.

South Rauceby

The public house (The Bustard) replaced, in 1860, an older inn, the Robin Hood, which stood at the south gate to the park, and a reading room was replaced by the village hall which residents of both North and South Rauceby use for their leisure pursuits.

⌘ RIGSBY

A delightful village on the edge of the Wolds with long views to the coast, Rigsby has one large farmhouse and a few smaller homes. A new house, modern, but in keeping with its surroundings, has recently been built on the site of an old condemned cottage. By its side a sty, home of many a fat pig, remains, protected by law, to tell its story of past rural life.

In the church of St James, built in 1865 to replace an earlier, burnt-down, thatched one, there is a 500 year old font and a Norman arch. A medieval helmet and sword, hanging near, take one's thoughts back to the days when the parish was of much importance and Gilbert of Rigsby was lord of the manor. A report of his judicial court records that one parishioner, who committed the offence of not sweeping his causey (causeway) was in mercy of the lord, fined two pence – not then the paltry sum it is today.

The adjoining hamlet of Ailby has a charming, low, thatched farmhouse and just three or four cottages. Two maintained footpaths link Rigsby, Ailby and Alford.

One of the long views to be seen from the village of Rigsby

Rigsby Wood has been for some years a nature reserve and now is of great interest to visitors on open days.

⌘ RUSKINGTON

Ruskington is 16 miles south of Lincoln on the 'old way of the towns' formerly used by hawkers, which passes through 13 villages between Sleaford and Lincoln. White's 1856 directory describes it as a large village upon a plain, with a fine stream of water running through it. It is now one of the largest villages in the county with a very long history. A prehistoric route from the Wolds to the Ancaster Gap which passed through the present parish is known, as well as the line of a Roman road seen in aerial photographs.

The village appears in the Domesday Book of 1086 as Reschintone. At that time there were 38 families, three water mills, a church and a priest. The lord of the manor owned twelve teams of oxen. The Norman church has had alterations and additions made down through the centuries. The spire was never replaced after falling down 300 years ago. In 1566 the churchwardens reported that some handbells which belonged to the church in Queen Mary Tudor's time had gone 'wee knowe not howe'.

A map of 1758 shows the layout of the streets very similar to the present day, with the stocks for malefactors, a workhouse, tithe barn, a pound for stray animals and fords in the beck. The fords have been replaced by bridges but the beck is still there with ducks swimming on it, and daffodils planted by the children among the cherry trees. There is an old saying that you are not a true Ruskingtonian until you have fallen in the beck.

During the Second World War army vehicles were parked under the trees by the beck. Many troops were billeted in Ruskington, and a memorial in the church and a new road named Arnhem Avenue commemorate the soldiers who trained here. Those who never returned are still remembered at the annual reunion of veterans and a service in the parish church.

⌘ SAXILBY-WITH-INGLEBY

Saxilby-with-Ingleby, six miles north-west of Lincoln on the A57, where you can arrive by car, bus, train or boat! The village population has grown from less than 400 in 1800 to almost 3,500 today.

The parish church on the northern edge of the village is dedicated to the Benedictine abbot St Botolph, great traveller and missionary. Built on the highest ground in the village, 57 ft above sea level, the oldest part of the church is the north

The Sun Inn at Saxilby, alongside the canal, is said to be haunted

aisle with its Norman door. The lofty Perpendicular style forms the remainder of the church. The tower, a copy of the original, was rebuilt in 1908 and dedicated by Bishop Edward King.

Before Saxulf and the Danes invaded, the Romans were very active in the area; coming to Saxilby along the Foss Dyke canal you are following in their footsteps! They extended the use of the river Witham at Lincoln by digging the Foss Dyke to link with the river Trent at Torksey Lock, giving them trading access to the Midlands and Humber estuary. Today the canal-side (Bridge Street) is a hive of activity. In 1987, the south side of the canal was repaired, and there are now picnic sites and conservation areas, and riverside walks and seats. A former railway footbridge, from Claypole, crosses the water giving easy access to the moorings and other amenities.

On Bridge Street, the Sun Inn is said to be haunted. Tom Otter, a local poacher/ labourer, married his wife Mary in 1806, then murdered her the same day. After the trial and execution his body was hung from a gibbet in Tom Otter's Lane about one mile outside the village. The legend is that on the anniversary of the deadly deed, ghostly noises and movements are heard.

⌘ SCAMBLESBY

The village nestles in a valley of the Lincolnshire Wolds, designated as an Area of Outstanding Natural Beauty, mid-way between Louth and Horncastle.

Scamblesby nestles amongst the Lincolnshire Wolds

Agriculture is the main industry, the acreage amounting to 2,002 acres, and the chief landowners being the Church Commissioners.

The village is very fortunate to have a junior and infants school, with an excellent staff committed to the welfare and well-being of the pupils, together with a Parent Teachers Association.

The County mobile library service is a great asset to the village. The 147 mile long Viking Way which passes through the village was opened in 1976 and stretches from Barton-upon-Humber to Oakham in Rutland.

The Methodist church was built in 1835, and extended in 1868. A new church was built on the site in 1977 and the official opening took place in January 1978. St Martin's church is built of stone with chancel, nave and a turret containing one bell; the register dates from 1569. The font has a massive and unusual bowl, and there are 18 bench ends, with faces peeping from fleur-de-lys poppy heads.

⌘ SCOTTER

Scotter stands almost half way between Scunthorpe and Gainsborough on land which slopes gently to the river Eau. Mention is made of Scotter in the Domesday Book and records reveal that in 1190 King Richard I granted the right to hold a market and fairs. The reign of King John gave Scotter a confirmation charter and a visit from his Majesty in 1216. The King, trying to raise an army to repel the threatened French invasion, stayed in the inn facing the village green. The landlord of the inn, as a mark of honour to his visitor, redesigned his inn sign and incorporated the badge on the shield of the Officer in Charge – a sun and an anchor. The present hostelry stands on the same site and the 'Sun and Anchor' is thought to be unique among inn names.

St Peter's church occupies a prominent position overlooking the village centre. Its history goes back to the 7th century. Above the present belfry door are the Ringers' Rules, in black and red Elizabethan lettering.

The main industries of Scotter have always been rural in nature and there is reference in historical records to three mills. One of these, in use until 1939, still stands. The Tower Mill was originally a post mill, built in the 15th century, and would have been essential to the agriculture of the surrounding area. Today's businesses relate to the service industries, of which there is a good variety.

One of the more widely known of Scotter's activities is its Silver Band, which provides entertainment over a wide area. It also takes part in competitions with some success. The truly rural character of our village can be seen on a pleasant Sunday evening in the summer when the band plays to a gathering on the riverside.

⌘ SIBSEY

Travellers along the A16 are following in the footsteps of prehistoric travellers along a sand and gravel ridge left by glaciers. Stretching from High Ferry, where it surfaces, to the Lincolnshire Wolds, this ridge connects the villages of Sibsey, Stickney and Stickford.

The original Sibsey was a Saxon settlement 'Siba-ey', the 'ey' meaning island so it was the Island of Siba. The island referred to cultivated land used for some grain and grazing, surrounded by wetlands which would have been dry in summer. Sibsey appears in the Domesday Book as Sibolci.

An example of Sibsey's rural history is the pinfold next to the A16 where stray cattle would have been impounded by the Pinder in the 18th century. He charged fines to the owners of the animals and had to pay double if his own animals were guilty! It is known that there were nearly 4,000 cattle and numerous sheep in the West Fen in the 1780s.

A feature of Sibsey is the Trader Mill, a six-sailed windmill in working order. People can see it in its full glory on open days each summer thanks to English Heritage. It was constructed in the 1870s from local clay bricks on the site of a previous post mill.

One local celebrity was Annie Besant, who was the wife of the vicar until she went to work in London late in the 19th century. As one of the first trades unionists she was a negotiator for the Matchgirls in their dispute in 1888 with their employers, Bryant and May.

Arthur Lucan, better known as Old Mother Riley on both stage and screen, was born in Sibsey in 1885 and lived in the village for many years.

⌘ SKELLINGTHORPE

About the time Lincoln Cathedral was being built, Skellingthorpe was a small hamlet on the high ground of the fen area west of Lincoln. Inhabitants either worked the land or made use of the many rabbit warrens which abounded on the poor soil. 'Skellingthorpe Duck' was said to be a London delicacy, so no doubt rabbits and ducks gave some people a meagre living.

Henry Stone was lord of the manor, who, lacking an heir, in 1693 bequeathed the land to Christ's Hospital, London. His coat of arms appears on the Stone Arms public house, which was in the area flooded to a depth of 6 ft when the Spalford bank burst in the 1700s. Farmers' wives travelled by boat to Lincoln market for three weeks until the waters subsided.

With the coming of day schools in the 1850s all landowners paid a tithe to the Spital Charity, which donated £50 for the 'poor and needy' of the parish. Nowadays a bible is traditionally given to every pupil leaving the village school from this fund.

In 1896 the railway arrived. The Great Central opened for passengers and goods traffic running from coast to coast. The 'goods' were mainly fish from Grimsby and coal from the Midlands. The station closed in September 1955 and

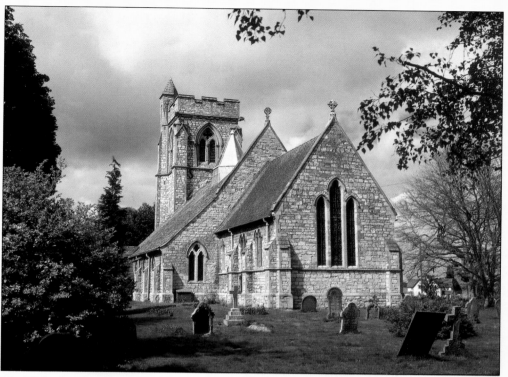

The village church in Skellingthorpe

on the site now stands a community centre and a youth hall. The old lamplighter's hut has been retained as a council store – but it still smells of paraffin!

Skellingthorpe was one of the largest parishes in England; the western boundary skirts the Nottinghamshire border and the 'Old Wood' is reputed to be the edge of Sherwood Forest.

⌘ SNARFORD

A scattered hamlet nine miles north of Lincoln, Snarford is notable for its church of St Lawrence, a stone building in Norman, Early Perpendicular and Decorated styles.

Inside are the wonderful tombs more reminiscent of a cathedral than a small church in a village where no evidence remains of any major residence. These are monuments to the St Poll or St Paule family. The earliest, 1582, is a canopied altar tomb bearing effigies to Sir Thomas St Poll and his wife. It is enriched by ten statuettes.

In a recess on the north wall and dated 1613 are two effigies representing Sir

Sir George St Pol and his wife Frances (nee Wray), church of St Lawrence, Snarford

George St Poll, Kt and Bart, and Frances his wife, with their daughter Mattathia and weeping cherubs. Frances reappears as the Countess of Warwick on a round tablet with her second husband, Baron Robert Rich of Leize, Earl of Warwick, who died in 1618. On a Latin-inscribed wall plaque a former Snarford parson tells us that Frances initially married at fifteen and after twelve years had a daughter Mattathia who died before her second birthday.

⌘ SOUTH ELKINGTON

The small village of South Elkington is situated on the A631 Louth/Market Rasen road. It is in an area of mixed farmland, on the eastern edge of the Wolds.

Many of the buildings in the village date from Victorian times when the village centred around Elkington Hall. Wander up Church Lane to All Saints church. You will pass the war memorial, which dates the First World War as ending in 1919; the school, closed in 1984 and now converted into a house; and the Church Institute, an attractive timbered hall, given to the village by a former vicar, Canon J. G. Smythe in 1905, and used for various functions.

The 13th century chalk and stone church was restored during the 19th century.

The chancel has a fine painted ceiling depicting the twelve apostles. In the well-kept graveyard, near the lychgate, grows an unusual thorny tree, the Honey Locust, planted to remind us of Christ's crown of thorns, and known as the Calvary Tree. It came from Palestine.

Elkington Vale is the old carriageway to the Hall and follows a wooded valley from the Lincoln Road. The whole area around South Elkington is endowed with a network of footpaths. So don a pair of walking boots and discover the sights and sounds for yourself. The seasons provide an ever changing tapestry, with perhaps the colours of autumn or waving corn of summer being the most spectacular.

Nearer to Louth is Thorpe Hall which borders the road and has an interesting tale to tell. In Elizabethan days it was the home of Sir John Bolle, a knight who fought at Cadiz, where he won the affection of a Spanish princess. The story goes that she followed him home, but seeing him happy surrounded by his family, she died, and her ghost, 'The Green Lady', haunts Thorpe Hall and its grounds.

⌘ SOUTH KYME

South Kyme stands on the river Slea, which flows through the flat Lincolnshire countryside. The fields now yielding a rich harvest of cereals and sugar beet once lay under water when the land was simply an undrained fen.

Kyme Eau, the waterway on either side of South Kyme, is home for leisure craft which pass by from the Witham Bottom lock, which has now been restored. A service is held once a year for the waterfolk, who tie up along the river side.

The 'Navigation' of the Slea can still be traced. Indeed you can't help but see the hump-backed bridge and the towpath which leads towards the church and tower, all that remains of the great castle which was built in the 14th century. It is said that a cow once rushed right up its stairs in fright. The moat and the fish ponds now stand dry, and are no longer used. It was thought at one time to have been the home of Robin Hood.

Without a car in South Kyme you cannot go far because there are very few buses. There is only one public house in the village, named the Hume Arms.

People have lived askirt this fen since the earliest times known to man, and will continue to live here – even though the County Council map shows that South Kyme is under water!

⌘ SPRINGTHORPE

In the lovely old church, which dates from Norman times, in the village of Springthorpe, you may uncover a sad little tale about a young woman known as Mary Hill. She died on Shrove Tuesday 1814 when ringing one of the four bells. She was carried up to the roof and then fell to the floor hitting a large stone, this now forms the base of the font. In a glass case just inside the Norman doorway you will find the Maiden's crown. This is one of three carried at her funeral by three maidens dressed in white. They also carried three garlands and three white gloves. These garlands when carried at the funeral of any unmarried girl were a symbol of chastity. You will also find the framed story on silk, and the Maiden's poem.

The church claims an entry in the Domesday Book and the oldest part, the tower, is reputed to be Saxon. The nave is 14th century and the herringbone masonry in the south wall indicates that the work was carried out in the 11th century. There is proof of the existence of the parish of Springthorpe since this time, supplied by the list of rectors who held this living.

Included in the parish is the hamlet of Sturgate, which is a short walk from the village.

⌘ STICKFORD

There was a community in Stickford in the days of William the Conqueror. His surveyors for the Domesday Book probably approached it along the slightly higher belt of dry land separating the East and West Fens. There was a ford on this road, probably spanning swamp, and it is from this high road and ford that the village took its name, which they recorded as 'Stitchesforde'.

The oldest parts of the parish church are thought to be early 13th century. Of special interest is the medieval great bell inscribed 'Sancte Gabriel'. In 1349, the Black Death hit Stickford and parish records show that four vicars died of it that year.

Eleven acres of land were once occupied by paupers of the village and at Sutton, near Alford, a two and a half acre pasture was let for £5.10s.0d a year, the money being given to the poor. In the late 19th century and early 20th century needy people, sometimes numbering 40 or more, used to line up at the vicarage door to receive Christmas relief. Poor relief is still administered, but the identities of recipients are now confidential.

There is a drain through Stickford, known as Catchwater Drain. In 1856, a Stickford resident, George Bycroft, ran a packet boat between Stickford and Boston. It left Stickford at 7 am on Wednesdays and Saturdays and returned at 3.30 pm. He carried both passengers and goods and moored the boat at Bargate Bridge, Boston. For many years, Isaac Hipkin and Son ran a large shop selling groceries, drapery and beer. They also sold coal, collected rates and kept cows. They owned teams of horses and travelled around Stickford and Stickford Fen selling provisions. Many customers, instead of paying cash for their goods, would barter for them with milk, eggs or butter.

⌘ STICKNEY

Stickney is situated midway between Boston and Spilsby on the main A16 road.

The church stands on a road junction beside the main road. It has a yew-shaded path up to the church door. The nave and base of the tower are 13th century with windows of the 15th century and a tower built at the beginning of last century.

The railway came to Stickney in 1912, and a tale is told of one day when the Paymaster came to pay the construction men and he slipped in the mud. His case with the wages in fell open and the wages – gold sovereigns – fell into the mud. There was quite a struggle to find them and a few were lost. The local lads could be seen for some time afterwards scrambling in the mud to find a sovereign to take home.

On the main roadside amongst the houses and between the two schools is the doctor's surgery, in a building which was once the Plough Inn public house. Opposite is the one remaining pub, The Rising Sun. Many years ago the landlord upset a regular who told him, 'I hope your Sun never rises again'. The reverse happened: it has remained open longest.

A short distance from the church towards Spilsby is the outdoor bowls club where excellent greens await the keen bowler. Residents like to congregate there on hot summer days to enjoy both the game and the company.

Close beside Stickney is the small parish of West Fen, where there is an eight acre field of hills and hollows and a pit. The silt soil was taken from this field many years ago to repair the roads when carts and farm waggons left ruts, long before tarmacadamed roads were made. A reminder of the history of this field is the name of the farm, Silt Pit Farm.

⌘ STURTON BY STOW

Sturton is eight miles north-west of Lincoln and the old Roman road, Tillbridge Lane, runs through the middle of the village.

There are several well preserved cottages in the village over 200 years old, notably on Tillbridge Lane. The Subscription Mill off Marton Road, a continuation of Tillbridge, was built in 1810.

St Mary's, Stow, is regarded as the 'Mother' of Lincoln Cathedral. It was built in Saxon times by the Bishops of Dorchester-on-Thames as a centre for the Church in Lincolnshire, and was endowed by Lady Godiva. After the Norman Conquest, when Lincoln acquired its own cathedral, St Mary's became simply a parish church (apart from a brief spell as a monastery). A major restoration was done by J. L. Pearson (architect of Truro Cathedral) in the 19th century. This included the roof and the elaborate vaulting in the chancel. The church also contains an ancient wall painting of Thomas à Becket.

Although a much larger village, Sturton by Stow has never had its own parish church. But Pearson, while restoring St Mary's, Stow, designed a simple red brick mission church for Sturton, which was built in 1879. It is called St Hugh's, in honour of the Bishop of Lincoln who lived (and kept his pet swan) at nearby Stow Park.

Sturton by Stow was the first village in the county to have a Methodist Society in 1771. John Wesley visited Sturton on 7th July 1779. A notable early Methodist, Sarah Parrott, who lived at Bracebridge, walked every Sunday to join the Methodists, meeting in various homes. Methodism reached Lincoln via Sturton, mainly due to the efforts of Sarah Parrott. A plaque to her can be seen in Sturton Methodist chapel, built in 1964.

⌘ SUTTON BRIDGE

Many people only know of Sutton Bridge as a bottleneck on the A17 but the swing bridge spanning the river Nene is the focal point of the village. It was opened in 1897, and replaced the earlier one built by such eminent engineers as John Rennie and Robert Stephenson to provide main road and rail routes across what had been a dangerous two mile estuary. Certainly the members of King John's baggage train found it to be hazardous as it is said that the King's Treasure is still lying somewhere in the area. The bridge is now a listed building.

Sutton Bridge has been associated with the RAF since 1926 when the first summer camp for airmen was opened; villagers soon became used to seeing the Blenheims, Spitfires, Hurricanes, Wellingtons and many other types of aircraft in the wide fenland skies of this area. Many Battle of Britain pilots trained here. In the

The swing bridge is the focal point of Sutton Bridge

village church of St Matthew, the altar in the north aisle is dedicated to the memory of those killed during their stay at the station and a tablet of oak carries all their names.

Other landmarks on the outskirts of the village are the two lighthouses flanking the river Nene. In the late 1920s Sir Peter Scott, the famous Director of Slimbridge Wildfowl Trust and one of the great nature conservationists of our time, lived in the East Bank Lighthouse. It was an ideal spot from which to study and paint the wild fowl which frequent the area.

One of Lincolnshire's famous poachers, Mr Mackenzie Thorpe, worked for Sir Peter. His adventures included clashes with the Royal gamekeeper at Sandringham and this interesting character attracted Prince Charles, who visited him at his council house and this led to the street being renamed Royal Close as a perpetual reminder.

⌘ SWAYFIELD

Swayfield is a small rural village of about 100 houses, some built of stone and some in brick, situated midway between the towns of Stamford, Grantham and Bourne. It has the distinction of lying on the highest ground traversed by the railway between London and the Scottish border. During the age of the steam engine, the straight length of railway track through the village was used to test the engines for speed and it is here that the famous 'Mallard' engine broke the speed record for steam engines.

The 12th century church of St Nicholas is set 200 yards from the rest of the village, the reason being that the original village houses were all burned to the ground in the 17th century after an outbreak of plague, to rid the area of infection.

Swayfield's other claim to fame is that it was here in 1588 that one of the beacons was lit in a chain across the country to warn of the threat of invasion by the Spaniards.

In the middle of the village is the Royal Oak public house. The oldest part of the pub, with its stone walls and oak beams, dates from the 17th century and it has been confirmed by historical records that Cromwell once stayed in 'the old inn at Swayfield'.

The village of Swayfield, situated as it is two miles from the A1 and less than an hour's drive from Lincoln, Nottingham, Leicester and Peterborough, has grown rapidly in the last few years, as more people working in cities seek sanctuary in the countryside for their homes and families. There remains a feeling of friendliness and community spirit in the village which has lost none of its rural charm.

⌘ SWINESHEAD

Swineshead lies six miles west of Boston on the edge of the fens and the village

The attractive market square of Swineshead

extends for over two miles along what was the A17 to Sleaford until the village was bypassed in 1985.

Swineshead takes its name from an inlet or channel called the Swin, which formerly ran up from the sea to the Market Place. The sea at one time being much nearer, the limit or head of the water was naturally called Swins Head – hence Swineshead.

A Cistercian abbey was founded here in the 12th century and was closed in 1536 at the Dissolution of the Monasteries. The site was granted to Edward Lord Clinton (later Earl of Lincoln).

Remains of a Danish encampment (a circular site called the Manwarings) is located north of Abbey Road. Roman relics have been unearthed nearby and there are traces of an early motte and bailey castle. It is thought salt pans were worked in what is known as Low grounds. Flint axe heads have also been found in the area.

Swineshead became a market town in the Middle Ages with a market held every Thursday. In the rather attractive market square the old stocks and butter cross are reminders of the village's status. Cheese Hill takes its name from the cheese sold on the site when the market was in existence. Tarry Hill was so called because a very large family lived in the vicinity, the records refer to the baptism of the 27th child of William and Sarah Tarry.

There are several attractive period houses in the village, two former windmills and near the square the parish church of St Mary the Virgin, built in the 13th century. Although the chancel was rebuilt in 1847 the rest of the church is of the Decorated period, and the handsome tower is capped by a lantern and short spire which are local landmarks.

⌘ TATTERSHALL WITH THORPE

Tattershall is a busy village, situated between the rivers Bain and Witham. Robert Tateshale gave his name to the place when he built a stone castle, forerunner of the present brick keep of Tattershall Castle, built by his son, also Robert.

This Robert gave King John a trained goshawk in return for the privilege of holding a weekly market, of which the market cross is now the only remnant. Today, the market place is often filled with cars, whose owners go to shop at what has laid claim to being the biggest village supermarket in the county.

The imposing brick keep of Tattershall Castle dominates the village and is a

The ancient Blue Bell hostelry at Thorpe is on a drover's road

landmark for many miles over the surrounding fens. For those who are agile enough to climb the unusual spiral stone staircase up to the summit, on a clear day there is the reward of seeing a wonderful panorama, as far as Lincoln Cathedral and Boston Stump. It now belongs to the National Trust, including a museum and gift shop in the guard house.

Holy Trinity church, a vast edifice, is close by the castle. In 1989, the 550th anniversary of this building, successor of an earlier place of worship, was celebrated by the restored and replaced great east window.

The village has a rich past, and is also prepared for the future. Lakes left from sand and gravel workings have been developed with surrounding land as a leisure centre, where caravanners spend holidays, fishing or at sport.

Thorpe is a hamlet on the road between Tattershall and Woodhall Spa. Mentioned in the Domesday Book as Torp, it was then superior in status. The Blue Bell Inn is an ancient hostelry on a drovers' road, and has a priest's hole, relic of the Civil War. Nature lovers have a wide scope at Thorpe, where Carr Wood is home to sand martins and other migratory birds among the sand and gravel workings, and where prehistoric remains have been found.

⌘ TEALBY

Tealby is set on the edge of the Lincolnshire Wolds, about mid-way between Lincoln and Grimsby. The Viking Way, a long distance footpath, passes through the village, which provides a welcome refreshment stop for walkers.

With the advantages of high ground and running water, it is thought to have been a settlement from earliest times. The hill on which the church stands was probably the site of a Saxon fort and the name itself shows its Viking origin. Under the name Tavelsbi, the village is mentioned in the Domesday Book and described as having four mills. In 1807 a ploughman turned up an earthen pot containing over 5,000 silver pennies dating from the reign of Henry II. Coins from the Tealby Hoard, as it is known, are now in many collections, including the British Museum and the Usher Art Gallery.

John Wesley records preaching at Tealby five times between 1747 and 1786. He describes the inhabitants as 'plain serious country people, very different from the wild unbroken herd to whom I preached at Horncastle in the evening'.

The beauty of the village comes from the golden limestone of the old cottages, the profusion and colour of the cottage gardens and the meandering stream, the river Rase, which skirts the village and is crossed by picturesque fords and bridges at each end. There is a fine Norman church, All Saints, and a rare thatched public house, the King's Head, dating from 1357.

Charles Tennyson, uncle of the poet, built a romantic Gothic castle, Bayons Manor, here between 1836–42. He also added the surname D'Eyncourt, recalling a remote ancestor. Unfortunately the house fell into disrepair after the Second

World War and was finally demolished in 1965. Later members of the family built the village hall, the Tennyson D'Eyncourt Memorial Hall, which was opened in 1930.

⌘ TETNEY

The village of Tetney is about two miles inland from the river Humber and the North Sea. Five or six miles away are the lovely rolling Lincolnshire Wolds. An urn containing Anglo-Saxon silver coins was unearthed in 1945 and that is considered evidence that Tetney existed as a dwelling place a thousand years ago.

It was for many years a farming community but that has changed over the years. Farming still goes on, but as the population has increased, most of its workforce travels to Grimsby, to the town itself and further along to the many factories along the Humber Bank. The village has a fine modern primary school, which replaced the old day school built by Methodists in 1856.

The ancient and beautiful church of St Peter and St Paul stands on the southern boundary, well tended and thriving. The Methodist chapel, St John's, stands in the centre of the village.

Not far from the church are the 'Blow Wells', several deep reservoirs of artesian water. Around these is a nature reserve of animals, birds and flowers, a very secluded and beautiful place.

Two miles away, on the coast lies the hamlet of Tetney Lock, through which flows the Navigation canal to the sea. At Tetney Lock is the RSPB bird sanctuary for many rare seabirds.

Along the Tetney Lock road are the enormous oil tanks served by the oil terminal on the coast. Oil is pumped through the 'Tank Farm' to the refineries inland.

⌘ THEDDLETHORPE

Theddlethorpe is a marsh coastal village with two parishes, St Helen's and All Saints. To the east of Theddlethorpe lies the sea and the dunes which form part of the Saltfleetby Nature Reserve, owned and administered partly by English Nature and partly by the Lincolnshire Wildlife Trust. The shoreline and dunes have been fashioned by centuries of wind and tide, depositing sand, flotsam and jetsam and building up sandbanks which are colonised by maritime grasses and plants and by the invasive and prickly sea buckthorn, which provide food for visiting migratory and resident birds.

At times the sand dunes are swiftly chopped away by the winter storms to leave a sheer 'cliff face' of sand; at other times there will be much more build up of sand bank than encroachment by the sea. On the older more established dunes, trees and bushes abound. As well as buckthorn there is hawthorn, wild rose, wild privet, elder

The church of St Andrew, Theddlethorpe

and even a few fruit trees and bushes unwittingly brought as seed by birds.

Theddlethorpe became a national landmark in 1972 when the North Sea Gas Terminal started its flow of gas into the national grid. Most people refer to the terminal as Conoco, but in fact there are two different companies in operation – the American based company Conoco, the original finder and developer of the 'Viking Field' bring the gas ashore and British Gas process it for industrial and domestic use and push it through to the national grid.

A famous visitor to Theddlethorpe was the writer D. H. Lawrence. The prospect pleased him and it fascinated him to walk on the wide shore; on one side the noisy restless waves ever changing and on the other side the silent, serene and sheltered sandhills.

⌘ THURLBY

Thurlby, as its name suggests, has Danish connections, and the beautiful and ancient church, although mainly Norman and Early English, shows earlier Saxon work. As the church stands on the bank of the Roman Car Dyke, a canal or catchwater drain which runs between Lincoln and Peterborough, it is possible that the church may have replaced a Roman shrine.

The church is dedicated to St Firmin, one of only two with this dedication in England and is well worth a visit. There is also a Methodist church, and the two work well together for the welfare of the village, especially in youth work.

Thurlby and its hamlet of Northorpe are now joined and there are two settlements to the south, Obthorpe and Kates Bridge, both of ancient origin.

A few years ago a very old woodland was lent and then sold to the Lincolnshire Trust for Nature Conservation and has been carefully looked after. It is known as Dole Wood and contains very old trees and plants and is open to the public occasionally. It is reached from Obthorpe Lane. More recently the same Trust has acquired the water meadows, known as slipes, on the banks of the river Glen which flows along the eastern boundary of the village between Thurlby and Baston Fens.

A few years ago two members of the Lawrence family, who own land in the village, gave a field to be used as a playing field. This land has been developed, and as well as a playing field there is a modern village hall and a new primary school. A cup was also given by these ladies to be presented annually to the person or group of persons who have done outstanding voluntary work for the benefit of the village.

⌘ UFFINGTON

Uffington's Lady Charlotte Bertie was a magnificent Victorian lady. Not only did she bear ten children in 13 years, but when her husband Joshua Guest died, she had no hesitation in taking over the ironworks herself. She spoke Italian and French, read Latin and Greek, and still found time to add medieval Welsh, Hebrew and Persian to her repertoire. And almost to the end of her life, she is said to have worked every day at knitting red woollen comforters for London cabbies.

Charlotte's ancestors came to Uffington in the 1670s having bought their estate from the dissolute second Duke of Buckingham. Their name lives on in the village's popular Bertie Arms Inn, parts of which are said to go back 300 years.

The Gainsborough Lady was a public house owned by the Trollope family until the 1970s and was formerly known as the Trollope Arms, a name which then caused little excitement. It blazed into local publicity again in 1986 when developers of new homes in the village rejected a suggestion to call the site Trollope Close. They feared its closeness to the word 'trollop' might make it difficult to sell the houses. In the end the district council backed up parish councillors who wanted to honour a family who had produced the great English novelist Anthony Trollope.

Despite the intrusion of the modern world, it is still possible to get away from workday pressures by one of the most pleasant of rural relaxations – walking along the meadows, lanes and river banks where blossom hangs lush in summer, berries abound in autumn, and where wild birds and animals reveal nature's richness at every season of the changing years.

⌘ UPTON & KEXBY

Upton is a village of ancient origin, four miles south-east of Gainsborough and 13 miles north of Lincoln. To the south is the neighbouring village of Kexby.

The parish church which stands impressively on slightly higher ground in the centre of Upton village replaces an early Norman church and is dedicated to All Saints and serves both villages. It contains six bells, the oldest dating to 1641.

In both villages, new housing blends well with the older mellow brick and tiled houses and farms. A number of Victorian buildings, including the old school, built with an attractive locally produced brick, give an interesting contrast and are a visible reminder of the thriving brick making business that once existed in Kexby.

Both villages have extensive field paths, all well signposted, leading to Heapham, Willingham, Knaith and Gainsborough, with magnificent views of the villages, the Trent valley and the Lincolnshire Cliff. The paths cross interesting fields, including some meadows where the pre-enclosure method of strip farming can still be traced.

In the centre of Kexby, facing the green, is the village well. Now preserved, the well, which is spring fed, was never known to run dry and in times of drought supplied water over a wide area. The spring may at one time have fed a small tributary of the river Till, which flows through low farmland to the east of both villages. Some historians are of the opinion that the Danes were able to navigate their boats along the Till to a mooring pool near the settlement. The river, now little more than a stream, is home for a variety of wildlife.

⌘ UTTERBY

The village of Utterby lies on the main A16 trunk road, four miles north of Louth. It is not recorded in the Domesday Book but almost certainly existed in earlier times, the name derived from the Danish 'Utter's Bye' meaning a habitation belonging to Utter.

The manor of Utterby was granted to Henry-de-Elye in 1220, and the name of Elye has been associated with the village for many centuries. The present manor house in Church Lane was built in 1639, and bears the coat of arms of the Elye family.

The present St Andrew's church probably originated in the 14th century, though the list of rectors displayed in the church goes back to 1220. This charming small church contains some interesting memorials, particularly the effigy of the 14th century rector William de Cumberworth, and a hatchment of William Davison dated 1702.

The ancient packhorse bridge in Utterby

Beyond the church is a 14th century packhorse bridge, thought to be one of only three in the country. This crosses a small stream, and was used in olden times by drovers bringing their animals from summer grazing on the marsh to market. A house nearby is still known as Drovers' Yard, where the drover and his animals could stay overnight. This bridge may also have been part of the salt route – packhorses carrying the salt from the coast to the inland towns. Holywell Lane, as its name implies, passes a holy well, which in ancient times was considered to have medicinal properties. Pilgrims who visited the well left their bandages on the surrounding bushes.

There are protection orders on the many fine trees in the village. The south side of the lane is within the Wolds Area of Outstanding Natural Beauty, and every effort is made to maintain this standard.

⌘ WADDINGTON

The Viking Way, which runs through Waddington, is a reminder that the Celts, farming the cliff top west of the Roman Ermine Street some 1,500 years ago, were overwhelmed by those warriors from the sea.

The Domesday Book reveals Waddington's development as an agricultural community. Signs of its medieval five fields system still show in furlong ridges by Milking Hill, later called 'Somerslay's Lane'. The farmers' homesteads were established in the well-drained, cliff-edge village itself, leaving the legacy of numerous fine houses and barns. A windmill stands on the southern cliff edge, a successor to a postmill that previously enhanced the northern boundary near the site of a Roman kiln.

The High Street and the Hilltop, running parallel from north to south, form the framework for the eleven linking lanes, which are at the heart of this well-wooded 'ladder' village. The majority of the houses date from the 16th century. Their roofs are bright with red pantiles, originally moulded from the clays of the vale below. Some stonewalled lanes still carry the names of early farmers, Timms and Capps, whilst Bartoft House reminds us of a prominent 13th century Norman knight.

To the east, lies the major RAF station of Waddington, opened in 1917 as a training centre for the Royal Flying Corps, and now at full strength and operating within the NATO Airborne Early Warning System. Since the extensive runway lies north to south, other villages bear a greater brunt of the noise overhead.

The presence of the station, which in 1959 received the Freedom of the City of Lincoln, is a great asset to village life. Not only is it generous with help and facilities, but the presence of its personnel makes feasible many activities and amenities within the village itself.

⌘ WELTON

The name of Welton by Lincoln distinguishes this parish from seven other Weltons in England. It is a charming village with a lot of the old houses built from locally made bricks of attractive colourings and Lincolnshire stone.

The Black Bull Inn and the church are centred around the village green. The old blacksmith's is now garages. The beck rises from Oldman head spring and meanders through the village and is now the home for many ducks. The original village pump still holds pride of place.

The church of St Mary which we know today has had extensions and improvements over the years. The first church was built in the 11th century, a second built in 1250, and it was then fully rebuilt in 1823. A giant boulder, a remnant from the Ice Age, stands by the porch.

Six prebends were given to Welton by Oliver Cromwell and some of the roads in Welton have been named after them – Brinkhall, Beckhall, Rivehall, Westhall and Painshall.

Saxon House, a community home, is so named as it is built on an old Saxon burial ground – remains were found in 1971 when foundations were being dug and they were later interred in the churchyard.

Welton is an expanding village with many houses built in recent years. The village hall, built in 1962 enjoys a thriving social calendar. To the rear is the bowling club, well attended by residents. A Sports and Social Club is situated in the playing field where members may play darts and pool as well as outdoor activities such as football and cricket, and there is also a children's playground.

⌘ WELTON LE MARSH

Welton le Marsh is a pretty village situated about seven miles from Skegness and five miles from Alford.

At one time a Roman road crossed part of the village but its name, which means 'land enclosed by trees', was first given to a Saxon settlement. The village is indeed very proud of its wood, extending to approximately one square mile. Until recently the oak stakes and posts from Welton wood were sought by farmers from a very wide area. In the middle of the wood is a large privately owned house known as Thwaite Hall. This stands on the site of an old castle and was at one time a monastic cell used by the monks of Thornton Abbey.

The church of St Martin in Welton le Marsh was rebuilt in 1792

At the north-east end of the village is a mound known as Castle Hill which is thought to date back to the Iron Age.

The Methodist chapel, still in use, was built in 1875 and is approached by a winding, ascending path. The parish church, dedicated to St Martin, was originally built of local white stone, but on 9th April 1791 the tower fell down, demolishing most of the church. Rebuilding commenced and a new church was opened in October 1792. In 1914 the original 14th century font was found in a field near the church being used as a cattle trough. This was restored and is much prized by the villagers.

There is a magnificent panoramic view from the old road leading westward towards the Louth road. On clear days it is possible to see as far as Mablethorpe to the north and Boston to the south, and even the cliffs of Hunstanton are visible.

⌘ WEST ASHBY

West Ashby is a village two miles north of Horncastle on the A153. It includes the hamlets of Midthorpe, Farthorpe and Furzehills (which was once known as Northorpe, a plague village). It appears as 'Aschebi' in the Domesday Book of 1086.

All Saints church is said to date back originally to the 13th century. The tower was extensively restored in 1871, as a memorial to the Victorian ballad writer Charlotte Alington Barnard, who composed under the pen name of 'Claribel'. It contains three bells (not in use) and eight tubular bells. In 1903 a clock was placed in the tower by Mr Basset in memory of his mother.

Around the walls of the church are a number of memorial tablets and perhaps the most interesting is the one in memory of one Richard Calthrop. Calthrop was a midshipman in the Royal Navy and fell at the battle of Algiers in 1816. The tablet gives, in unusual and dramatic detail, the story of the young hero's death, and is a vivid evocation of a naval action of those times.

Notable buildings in the village include the manor house built in 1840. The Grove, once the home of the Elmhirst family, is said to be home to several ghosts. West Ashby House is a Queen Anne mansion, formerly used by the Bishops of Carlisle. The front door and portico are said to have come from Captain Cook's house in London.

Sand and gravel were excavated near the river Bain, and the area has now been converted to a golf course. In 1977 archaeologists found a Bronze Age burial ground near the gravel pits at Furzehills.

⌘ WHAPLODE

Whaplode is a village situated five miles from Holbeach and eight miles from Spalding. It has changed a great deal over the last few decades.

The road by the post office once led to the end of the road and onto the highway, where there was a mill that ground the corn into flour and cattle feed. There were ten mills of this kind round Whaplode, as the fields held mainly grain and potatoes.

One old house in the village was once the harbourmaster's house, and people from the fens – 'Whaplode, St Catherine and Sutton St James' – had to pay a toll at the gate before they could get into Holbeach, as there used to be a waterway to the main road from the village. The monks from Crowland (or Croyland) came up the river by coracle from Stamford to build St Mary's church at Whaplode.

It is an 11th century church, so very grand but simple in its interior. Inside there is the 17th century Irby Tomb, where an effigy of Sir Anthony Irby and his wife lie with their children kneeling beside them. There is also a Methodist chapel in Whaplode and it was almost always full. There were farms around it and the voices of the farm labourers and their wives rang out on Sunday in competition with the church!

⌘ WICKENBY

Wickenby, known as Wichingbee in the Domesday Book, lies approximately eleven miles north-east of Lincoln and includes the hamlet of Westlaby.

It is a village scattered along the approach roads with large tracts of farmland in between and the beck running along one side.

The old manor house, now four dwellings, thought to have been built in the 15th/16th century, is a listed building. Part of the old moat can be seen across the fields, while on the Chapel Field opposite the results of ridge and furrow farming are still evident.

In Wickenby wood, mentioned in the Domesday Book, the habitat for numerous wild flowers has been preserved. The railway station, now disused, lies near the wood about half a mile from the centre of the village.

The ancient stone church of St Peter and St Lawrence is in the late Perpendicular style and was restored in 1878, when the tower was added. The Methodist chapel, built in the same year, was converted in 1972 into a remarkable little theatre, privately owned. It is known as the Broadbent Theatre. Here professional travelling companies present excellent modern theatre, while amateurs also produce plays of a high standard.

Wickenby airfield, built for and used in the Second World War by the Lancaster bombers, lies on the first rise above the Lincoln shelf. From it there is an excellent view of Lincoln Cathedral, especially ethereal when floodlit. The airfield is still used by a private flying club. On it there is an impressive memorial to the 1,080 men of No 1 Bomber Command, 12 and 626 Squadrons RAF Wickenby, who failed to return from their missions. It takes the form of Icarus with burnt wings falling from the sky and is made out of twisted bomber metal.

⌘ WITHAM ON THE HILL

Witham on the Hill was once known as Witham-Super-Montem. The parish church of St Andrew stands in the centre, and, as the village is on high ground, the spire is visible from a considerable distance. The church is a Norman stone building, and possesses examples of many styles of later architecture. The Norman font has an elaborate canopy, behind which is a small lancet window. Witham church has possessed a clock for over 400 years; this is one of the earliest instances known of a clock in a church tower dating back to before the invention of the pendulum.

The strange position of the tower, standing at the south and away from the nave, is a remarkable feature. The tower was rebuilt in 1738, after it had collapsed. The story is told in White's 1856 Directory of Lincolnshire: 'The spire with a great part of the tower fell down in 1738, whilst the ringers, having rung some merry peals, were regaling themselves in a neighbouring inn'.

Close to the church is the Victorian school room, built in 1847. It is now the

The old school house at Witham is now the church hall

church hall and is inscribed with the motto: 'Train up a child in the way he should go and when he is old he will not part from it'.

Palace Farm dates back to the 11th century, and was once the manor house, with villagers' huts and later houses clustered around it. The name is derived from its having been the former southern palace of the Bishops of Lincoln, being conveniently situated only a day's ride from Lincoln.

In a neighbouring field is a 17th century dovecote. Doves were kept as a food source, to be eaten either fresh or salted in the winter. Close to the church are the old stocks in a good state of preservation. However, the stocks were covered over in very recent times. The top bar was used in bonfire celebrations, to mark the relief of Mafeking during the Boer War, but luckily the rest was saved by the vicar of the time.

⌘ WOODHALL SPA

Woodhall Spa is situated almost at the centre of Lincolnshire. The road from Lincoln crosses the river Witham at Kirkstead Bridge and enters the village along the tree-lined Witham Road. The gravestones and the war memorial at the

The 'Kinema in the Woods' at Woodhall Spa has provided entertainment since 1922

crossroads mark the site of the first church to be built in the village, St Andrew's (1847–1957).

Over the crossroads and adjacent to the car park in Station Road is the memorial to 617 (Dambuster) Squadron, RAF. The memorial was dedicated in 1987 and is in the form of a breached dam. The squadron was based at the wartime airfield of Woodhall Spa shortly after the epic dams raid in 1943.

The now deserted Rheumatism Clinic enclosed the site of the first spa well. It was here, in 1821, John Parkinson of Bolingbroke started to sink a coal mine shaft. After some two to three years and various disasters the shaft was abandoned and covered over. Legend says that when the shaft flooded and overflowed, cattle drinking the water were cured of their ailments. Local inhabitants believed the water relieved the symptoms of rheumatism, gout and scurvy. The lord of the manor, Thomas Hotchkin, believed the water to be beneficial for his gout and built the first Pump Room and Bath House and the Victoria Hotel in 1839. Woodhall Spa was born.

In 1922, Captain Allport converted the cricket pavilion into the Pavilion Cinema with a back projection system. The cinema was the 68th cinema to be opened in the country and became known as the 'Kinema in the Woods'. It was patronised by members of the Royal family during their visits to nearby Petwood. Today, the cinema continues to provide regular entertainment for inhabitants and visitors by showing back projected, up to date, films and by live music from the theatre organ.

⌘ WOOLSTHORPE BY BELVOIR

Woolsthorpe by Belvoir is in Lincolnshire, but only just. The Leicestershire border is only yards away to the west and the Nottinghamshire border is about four miles to the north-west.

A pleasant place to live with open fields and woods all around. Visitors come from all over the world looking for Sir Isaac Newton's birthplace, which is at Woolsthorpe by Colsterworth, but once here they enjoy the scenery! It is confusing having two villages with almost the same name within ten miles of each other.

The church of St James was built in 1847 at a cost of £3,500. It stands about one mile from the original church, which was destroyed by the Roundheads during the Civil War when it is said that it was used to stable their horses overnight. On leaving the next morning the soldiers set fire to the straw and the church burned down.

The week commencing the first Sunday after the 5th of August has always been kept as Feast Week when visits home were made, a procession to church, dancing, a fair and Flower Show were held. Nowadays, only the Flower Show survives, and a children's sports afternoon. On Spring Bank Holiday Monday a street market is held to raise money for the village hall funds.

This is an estate village but since the 1970s some land has been sold and new houses built, including nine bungalows for senior citizens.

During the Second World War, Woolsthorpe Stables housed many soldiers, including the Durham Light Infantry, the Sherwood Foresters and the Royal Pioneer Corps. Two searchlight batteries were also stationed here.

⌘ WORLABY

Worlaby is a village of quiet peaceful charm, one of several between Brigg and Barton overlooking the carrs (the once marshy lowlands) of the broad Ancholme valley. From the main road the village rises up the hillside and, behind a parkland area of tall specimen trees, is dominated by the tall graceful tower of St Clement's church. The narrow tower arch is Saxon and there are many Gothic details, but most of what you see today is from a rebuilding of 1837.

Above the village are two notable artefacts. One is a handsome Victorian drinking fountain, erected in 1874 by Sir John Astley using left-over stone from

The village of Worlaby hides amongst the trees

the reconstruction of the church. It is fed continuously by a nearby spring. The other is a striking bronze statue of a kneeling nude entitled 'Emancipating Andromeda', encountereed as you ascend out of the village.

Set back from the main road at the foot of the village are the impressive model farm buildings of Worlaby House Farm, where the arch of the gabled façade is picked out in distinctive green and white hoops. Built in 1873 the farm is flanked by pairs of cottages originally built for the farm workers.

⌘ WRAGBY

Wragby is a pleasant community situated ten miles from Lincoln on the A158 road to Skegness. Settled originally by the Vikings, it is recorded in the Domesday Book of 1086.

The Market Place contains a number of old and interesting buildings. On the west side, concealed by a modern facade, is a hall house with cruck beams. On the east side is the old manor house and the ancient market hall. On the north side is a row of Regency buildings including the Turnor Arms, an old coaching inn. Other hostelries are the Adam and Eve (notable for its most interesting pub sign!) and the old Red Lion, which has been a private house for many years.

The Turnor family were generous and benevolent squires of the Panton estate, including Wragby, from the late 17th century until the sudden death of the Squire during the First World War, when the estate was broken up and sold. In 1698 the Turnor family founded the Turnor's Square hospital and chapel for six clergy widows and six other poor widows or widowers.

In 1836 the church, built in 1200, was in a dilapidated state and Christopher Turnor and 38 other residents petitioned the Bishop of Lincoln for its demolition and for the erection of a new church on land given by Christopher Turnor himself. He also gave £2,000 of the £3,500 which the building cost. The new church in modern Gothic style was consecrated on 4th April 1839. Six bells from the old church were hung in the new belfry. Three of these were cast in Nottingham in 1697 and the other three from the same foundry were brought from Kirmond-le-Mire.

Adjacent to the site of the old church and burial ground is the Routland (tournament place). Ancient earthworks mark the place where Countess Judith, niece of William the Conqueror and resident in Wragby, may well have lived in a manor house surrounded by a timber stockade.

⌘ WRANGLE

Wrangle is situated off the A52, only a short distance from the shores of the Wash. It was spelled Weranghe in the Domesday Book, and in the 15th century, Wranghill. The church of St Mary and St Nicholas is built in the late Norman and

Early English style with later additions. It has a fine pulpit of the Elizabethan period and a tower with six bells.

Wrangle was quite an important village in the 13th and 14th centuries, with a thriving market held on Saturdays. In 1359 when Edward III was raising a navy to invade France, this village was one of 82 places in the kingdom asked to send help. Wrangle sent one ship and eight men, more than Liverpool who only sent one ship and five men.

The bedehouse and school were founded in 1555 by Thomas Alenson. He gave his house at Joy Hill to be converted into a bedehouse for three poor men and two poor women, one of whom should be able to instruct the children in English and Latin. In 1705 Rev William Erskine gave nine acres of land, the rent from which was used to make up the weekly salaries and stipends of the five members of the bedehouse, and also to pay the schoolmaster.

The bedehouse at Wrangle

Many human bones were dug up in a part of the village called Gallows Marsh. In 1852 an ancient brass ring, once thickly gilded, was found in the vicarage garden, engraved 'en bon an'. It is thought to have been a New Year gift, dating from the late 15th century.

Joseph Gilbert, a member of an old Wrangle family associated with the area for over 75 years from the middle of the 18th century, was attached to the second expedition under Captain Cook. He gave his name to a small, desolate island near Tierra del Fuego, and it is still called Gilbert's Isle to this day.